Modern Business Management

Xinwei Cao

Modern Business Management

palgrave
macmillan

Xinwei Cao
School of Business
Jiangnan University
Wuxi, China

ISBN 978-981-96-0593-4 ISBN 978-981-96-0594-1 (eBook)
https://doi.org/10.1007/978-981-96-0594-1

This Palgrave Macmillan imprint is published by the registered company Springer Nature Singapore Pte Ltd.
The registered company address is: 152 Beach Road, #21-01/04 Gateway East, Singapore 189721, Singapore

Preface

In an era marked by globalization and rapid technological advancements, the landscape of market competition is undergoing profound changes. Traditional industries, dominated by giants who have accumulated capital, controlled supply chains, and fostered brand loyalty, are leveraging the power of compounding to amplify even the smallest advantages over time, eventually securing a firm grip on the market. This "winner-takes-all" phenomenon is prevalent across various sectors, including manufacturing, technology, and the internet industry. However, does this mean that emerging enterprises are destined to merely survive in the gaps? This book is written to answer that very question.

Through an interdisciplinary lens, combining insights from evolution theory, biology, computer science, and economics, this book delves deeply into the phenomena of market competition. By drawing analogies to the principle of "survival of the fittest" in evolution, we explore how businesses can adapt and evolve in a complex and ever-changing market environment. Just as organisms optimize their physiological characteristics to cope with environmental changes during evolution, companies must enhance their competitiveness through technological innovation, management optimization, and strategic market adjustments. These analogies not only offer readers a unique perspective but also reveal the common patterns in the development of both traditional and emerging industries.

In its detailed analysis, the book discusses how traditional industry giants consolidate their market positions by controlling supply chains, accumulating capital, and fostering brand loyalty. It also borrows from the "heartbeat hypothesis" in biology to reveal the relationship between rapid market iteration and the business life cycle. Through these analogies, we gain a deeper understanding of the challenges and opportunities that companies face at different stages of their development.

More importantly, this book offers strategies for emerging enterprises. How can small companies stand out in fiercely competitive markets dominated by giants? The answer lies in deepening their focus on niche markets, building technological barriers, and consistently emphasizing innovation. With these efforts, small companies can, like the "dark horse" in evolution, rapidly rise in specific fields and even disrupt existing market structures.

Furthermore, the book highlights the importance of choosing and applying the right management models. At different stages of development, companies should flexibly use management tools like Key Performance Indicators (KPIs) and Objectives and Key Results (OKRs), based on their unique characteristics, to enhance organizational execution and innovation capabilities. Drawing from the concept of long-term adaptation in biology, the book argues that deep accumulation and a commitment to long-termism are key to overcoming internal and external challenges. In a fast-changing market, only those companies that can continuously innovate and quickly adapt to market changes will truly gain a competitive edge.

This book is designed primarily for entrepreneurs and business professionals who are navigating the complexities of competitive markets. Special attention is given to those operating in or collaborating with Chinese businesses, providing insights that can be applied across both global and local contexts. I hope this book provides readers with interdisciplinary insights, whether you are in a traditional industry or an emerging field, to inspire you and help you find the right path for your company's survival and development. Let us explore the challenges and opportunities of the era of over-competition together and find ways to break through in the fierce market competition.

Wuxi, China Xinwei Cao

Contents

1 The Entrenchment of Traditional Industries and the Winner-Takes-All Phenomenon 1

1.1 The Entrenchment of Traditional Industries: An Unbreakable Market Structure 1

1.2 The Winner-Takes-All Phenomenon and Its Internal Mechanisms 3

1.3 Winner-Takes-All and the Advantages of Giants 5

1.3.1 Case Study: Tech Giants and the Winner-Takes-All Phenomenon in the Internet Industry 7

1.4 Better to Be a Big Fish in a Small Pond: Dominating Niche Markets over Struggling in Mainstream Industries 8

References 11

2 The Dark Horse of New Tracks and the Life-Death Cycle 13

2.1 Starting with the Billion Heartbeats of Mammals 13

2.2 The Lifespan-Heartbeat Hypothesis: Implications for Us 15

2.3 Slowing Down to Outpace: The Wisdom of the New Era 16

2.4 Persisting in Long-Termism 19

References 21

3 Don't Put All Your Eggs in One Basket vs. Going All-In on a Single Venture 23

3.1 The Contrasting Investment Philosophies 23

3.2 The Role of Confidence in Information and Forecasting 25

3.3 Confidence in Information and Predictions 27

3.4 Don't Earn Beyond Your Knowledge 29

3.5 Achieving High Returns with Low Risk 30

References 32

4 Top-Down Management vs. Bottom-Up Innovation 33

4.1 KPI vs. OKR 33

4.2 Military-Style Management vs. the Emergence of Innovation 36

4.3 Autocratic Management with KPI vs. Democratic Management with OKR 37

4.4 Choosing the Right Metrics at Different Stages of Development 38

4.5 Does My Company Also Need to Learn from IBM's Management Model? 39

References 41

5 Efficient Traditional Industries vs. Inefficient Emerging Industries 43

5.1 The "Efficiency" Behind Tech Giants: High Barriers and Excess Profits 43

5.2 The Efficiency Kings of Traditional Industries: Intensification and Competitive Compression 44

5.3 Market Opportunities from Corporate Management: The Battle Between High-Barrier and Low-Barrier Industries 45

5.4 Why Big Companies Can Tolerate Inefficiency and Even Overstaffing 45

5.5 The Three Stages of Industry Development 46

5.6 Choosing the Right Time to Enter 48

References 50

6 The Contraction of Primary and Secondary Industries vs. the Expansion of the Tertiary Industry 51
6.1 The Contraction of Primary and Secondary Industries 51
6.2 The Expansion of the Tertiary Industry 53
6.3 Career Choices for the Future 53
References 56

7 Moore's Law and Endless Desires 59
7.1 Moore's Law: Growth on the Supply Side 59
7.2 The Unbounded Desires: Growth on the Demand Side 61
7.3 The Escalation of Imbalance 61
7.4 The Paradox of Desire and Technological Progress 63
7.5 The Desire-Driven Cycle 64
References 64

8 The Moore's Law in the Field of Artificial Intelligence 67
8.1 ChatGPT: The Dark Horse of 2023 and the Dawn of a New Era in AI 67
8.2 The Growing Gap Between Human and AI Intelligence 70
8.3 Reflections on the Future: Optimism or Worry? 71
8.4 Re-examining Human Existence 73
8.4.1 The First Setback: Copernicus's Heliocentric Theory 73
8.4.2 The Second Setback: Darwin's Theory of Evolution 73
8.4.3 The Third Setback: Freud's Psychoanalysis 75
8.4.4 The Fourth Setback: The Rise of Artificial Intelligence 75
8.5 Reconsidering Humanity 76
References 78

9 Lessons from the Extinction of Dinosaurs 79
9.1 A Historical Review of Dinosaur Extinction 79
9.2 Economic Transformation: Lessons from Dinosaur Extinction 80
9.3 Contemporary Revelations 84
9.4 Is Bigger Always Better? 85
References 87

10 The Boundaries of AI Capabilities 89
10.1 Is AI Omnipotent or Limited? 89
10.2 Escaping the Risk of Being Replaced by AI 93
References 96

11 The Evolution from Mental Labor Today to Physical Labor Tomorrow 97
11.1 The Glory Days of the Past 97
11.2 The Rise of Autonomous Driving and the Decline of the Driving Profession 100
11.3 Is Programming Still Attractive? 103
11.4 Re-assessing: Today's Mental Labor Degrades into Tomorrow's Physical Labor 106
References 108

12 One Step Ahead Is a Pioneer, Two Steps Ahead Is a Martyr 109
12.1 Disproportionate Contribution and Reward 109
12.2 Entrepreneurial Choices: When All Is Ready, All That's Missing Is the Final Push 112
References 115

13 A Makeshift Troupe Performing a Grand Opera: The Startup Path of Emerging Companies 117
13.1 The World as a Makeshift Troupe 117
13.2 Imperfection in the Early Stages Is the Norm 119
13.3 The Growth Story of Youth: The Dominant Role of Core Elements 121
13.4 Core Elements Driving Other Factors 123
References 125

14 Company Strategy Choices: Rapid Expansion vs. Quality Over Quantity 127
14.1 r/K Selection Theory in Ecology 127
14.2 r/K Selection Theory and Company Strategy Choices 128
14.3 Case Studies: Rapid Expansion vs. Quality and Sustainability 131
14.4 Individual-Level Rapid Expansion vs. Quality and Sustainability Strategies 132
References 134

15 Re-thinking the Theory of Evolution 135

15.1 Survival of the Fittest: The Fittest Are Not Necessarily the Strongest 135

15.2 The 35-Year-Old Crisis for Technologists 137

15.3 Artificial Evolution and Franchising 139

15.4 The Driving Force of Evolution 142

References 144

Epilogue 147

Index 149

List of Figures

Fig. 1.1	Traditional industries reach market dominance through control over supply chains, capital accumulation, and brand loyalty, eventually becoming industry giants	2
Fig. 1.2	Winners accumulate most of the resources and wealth, while smaller competitors or failures receive relatively insignificant portions	6
Fig. 1.3	The "Better to Be a Big Fish in a Small Pond" concept emphasizes the superior profits that companies in niche markets can achieve by leading their sector	9
Fig. 2.1	The shrew's heart rate may reach 1,200 to 1,500 beats per minute, yet it lives only 1 to 2 years. The blue whale's heart rate is just 5 to 10 beats per minute, but it can live for 70 to 80 years. However, both species experience a similar number of total heartbeats over their lifetimes	14
Fig. 2.2	Different animals have varying lifespans—turtles and whales have long lifespans, while some insects, like mayflies, live only for a few hours to a few days in their adult stages, echoing Zhuangzi's sentiment of "life and death in a single moment"	17
Fig. 2.3	Focused deep work vs. trend chasing. On the left, a farmer concentrates on cultivating crops, while on the right, market chaos ensues as people constantly switch industries in blind pursuit of the next big thing	18

Fig. 2.4	Long-termism: The power of patience and accumulation. The tree grows strong and full over time, nurtured by a gardener's careful attention, from sapling to lush, mature tree	20
Fig. 3.1	Should you put all your eggs in one basket?	24
Fig. 3.2	Understanding diversification vs. concentration through predicting the landing point of a cannonball	27
Fig. 3.3	Risk and return often appear contradictory. However, in familiar fields, it is possible to achieve low risk and high returns	31
Fig. 4.1	KPIs vs. OKRs	34
Fig. 5.1	Industry development includes three stages: R&D-driven stage, intensification stage, market leader stage	49
Fig. 6.1	Machines replace human jobs as technological progress leads to higher efficiency	52
Fig. 6.2	Changing career preferences among future graduates: fields related to the primary and secondary industries are gradually losing appeal, while those related to the tertiary sector are becoming more popular	55
Fig. 7.1	Moore's Law illustrates how hardware performance, including integrated circuits, has exponentially increased over time	60
Fig. 7.2	The unbounded expansion of human desires, such as our pursuit of more health, rights, love, freedom, and happiness	62
Fig. 8.1	General AI technology, represented by ChatGPT, is drastically impacting and reshaping our lives	68
Fig. 8.2	Large language models, represented by ChatGPT, have successfully passed the Turing Test in various scenarios, heralding a new era	69
Fig. 8.3	As AI intelligence increases, human intelligence faces potential threats, with many worrying about whether AI will eventually subjugate humanity	71
Fig. 8.4	Copernicus's heliocentric theory, Darwin's theory of evolution, Freud's psychoanalysis, and the rise of AI surpassing human intelligence have all dealt significant blows to humanity, severely undermining our confidence	74
Fig. 9.1	Before the asteroid impact, dinosaurs were at the top of the food chain, dominating the ecosystem. Their large size and strength were fully displayed in that era, similar to how companies pursue expansion, listing, and capital accumulation during periods of economic growth	80

Fig. 9.2 After the asteroid impact, dinosaurs struggled in the harsh environment, weakened by food shortages and starvation. This scenario mirrors the bleak atmosphere of an economic downturn, highlighting the dinosaurs' powerlessness in the face of extreme survival challenges 81
Fig. 9.3 Bigger is not always better; sometimes being small and specialized is more advantageous than being large and strong. The environment ultimately determines which is better 87
Fig. 10.1 AI has many limitations 92
Fig. 10.2 Actively engaging in fields where AI struggles can help avoid the risk of being replaced by AI 95
Fig. 11.1 The profession of driving had a certain technical threshold and was once widely regarded as a skill-intensive occupation 99
Fig. 11.2 The advent of autonomous driving poses a serious threat to the driving profession. Public perception of the driving industry is also undergoing significant changes, with the technical threshold of driving increasingly seen as low, and the profession more as low-skill manual labor 101
Fig. 11.3 Programmers are gradually shifting from white-collar mental labor to what some call "IT laborers" engaged in manual labor 104
Fig. 11.4 Today's mental labor gradually degrades into tomorrow's physical labor 107
Fig. 12.1 Those who deliver the final "kick" often reap the greatest rewards, while those who laid the foundation may not receive the recognition or rewards they deserve from the market 111
Fig. 12.2 The best time to enter is when all is ready and only the final push is needed 114
Fig. 13.1 The world is a giant makeshift troupe 118
Fig. 13.2 Rome wasn't built in a day. Many companies lack key elements in their early stages, but that doesn't prevent them from eventually achieving greatness 120
Fig. 13.3 Dominant elements compensate for and supplement other deficiencies, allowing a seemingly makeshift troupe of a company to eventually overcome its shortcomings and become strong 124

Fig. 14.1 Mice and flies adopt the rapid expansion strategy, relying on "winning by numbers," they can quickly expand their populations in a short time, adapting to rapidly changing environments. In contrast, elephants, whales, and humans are typical quality over quantity strategists, meticulously nurturing and caring for each offspring to improve survival rates 129
Fig. 14.2 The rapid expansion strategy solves problems through broad exploration and quick action, while the quality over quantity strategy addresses issues through careful nurturing and deep incubation 133
Fig. 15.1 Darwin's theory of evolution illustrates the harsh survival competition in nature where natural selection determines survival 136
Fig. 15.2 The 35-year-old crisis 138
Fig. 15.3 The unusual evolution of fainting goats and goldfish is the result of artificial selection 141
Fig. 15.4 Darwin's theory of survival of the fittest and Malthus's population theory are equally applicable in the business world. The conflict between limited resources and unlimited demand, market competition among enterprises, and the concept of "survival of the fittest" together create the conditions for successful companies to stand out in competition 143

CHAPTER 1

The Entrenchment of Traditional Industries and the Winner-Takes-All Phenomenon

1.1 The Entrenchment of Traditional Industries: An Unbreakable Market Structure

In the global economic system, traditional industries have undergone decades, or even centuries, of development, gradually forming an unbreakable market structure. Industry giants have solidified their market position by continuously optimizing supply chains, accumulating capital, and expanding market share. This long-term accumulation of advantages has led to the entrenchment of industry hierarchies, meaning that once a giant company establishes its dominance, it becomes extremely difficult for new entrants to disrupt the existing industry structure unless a major disruption occurs (Fig. 1.1).

The advantages of giant companies are reflected in several aspects. First, they typically control the entire supply chain, from raw material procurement to production and finally to sales, all of which are managed at the lowest cost and with maximum efficiency. For example, Procter & Gamble (P&G) ensures low-cost raw material supply through long-term partnerships and large-scale purchasing while optimizing production processes to improve manufacturing efficiency.

Second, control over sales channels is another key advantage for giant companies. Over years of market expansion, these companies have built extensive and deeply penetrated sales networks. These networks include not only offline retail but also e-commerce platforms and emerging online

X. Cao, *Modern Business Management*,
https://doi.org/10.1007/978-981-96-0594-1_1

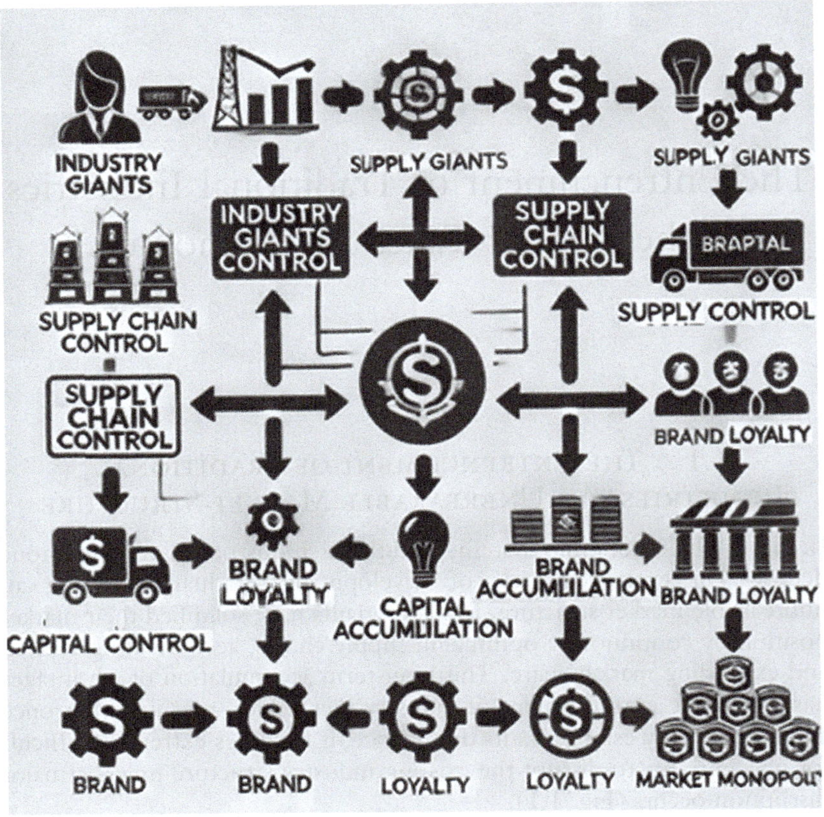

Fig. 1.1 Traditional industries reach market dominance through control over supply chains, capital accumulation, and brand loyalty, eventually becoming industry giants

sales channels. Leveraging these channels, giants can quickly capture market share and promote new products, while new entrants face significant challenges and costs to access these channels. For example, P&G products are sold in virtually all major supermarkets and retailers worldwide, making it extremely difficult for new brands to gain access to these channels.

Giant companies enjoy strong brand recognition in the minds of consumers, further reinforced by advertising, promotions, and customer service efforts. This brand loyalty means that consumers often default to these well-known brands when making purchases, while new entrants struggle to gain a significant market share.

Capital accumulation and economies of scale also provide giant companies with a competitive edge. This allows them to make large-scale investments, operate with optimal cost structures, and withstand price wars in the market. For example, P&G has continuously expanded its product lines and strengthened its market control through acquisitions and integration of other brands, solidifying its dominant position in the industry.

These advantages present enormous challenges for new entrants in traditional industries. New companies not only need to invest significant capital and time in building supply chains and sales channels, but they also need to continuously invest in brand building to educate and attract consumers. However, consumer brand loyalty makes it difficult for new brands to break through unless they offer highly differentiated products or services, which is often challenging in an industry dominated by giants.

New entrants also tend to have weaker capital strength and lower risk tolerance, making them more vulnerable to market fluctuations or policy changes. In contrast, giant companies can maintain stability through diversified investments and risk hedging, even further consolidating their market position during crises. In many mature traditional industries, a few giant companies have gradually formed a "winner-takes-all" scenario by leveraging their long-term market advantages. The vast majority of the industry's profits are concentrated in the hands of a few giants, while smaller companies are marginalized, making it difficult for them to share in the industry's growth.

1.2 The Winner-Takes-All Phenomenon and Its Internal Mechanisms

We can illustrate the "winner-takes-all" phenomenon with a simple mathematical model. Suppose there are five companies in the restaurant industry: Company 1, Company 2, Company 3, Company 4, and Company 5. Each company has a different profit margin—5%, 10%, 15%, 20%, and 25%, respectively. Initially, each company is worth 1 million, and their market share is equally divided at 20%. Over time, the compounding effect changes the value of these companies after 10 years as follows:

- Company 1: 100 (1 + 5%)^10 = 162.89
- Company 2: 100 (1 + 10%)^10 = 259.37
- Company 3: 100 (1 + 15%)^10 = 404.56
- Company 4: 100 (1 + 20%)^10 = 619.17
- Company 5: 100 (1 + 25%)^10 = 931.32

While the market value of each company has increased, the distribution of market share has changed significantly. After 10 years, the total market value is 2377.31, and the market shares of Company 1 to Company 5 are:

- Company 1: 6.86%
- Company 2: 10.91%
- Company 3: 17.00%
- Company 4: 26.03%
- Company 5: 39.20%

As time progresses, the gap continues to widen. For example, after 20 years, the market shares are:

- Company 1: 1.66%
- Company 2: 4.21%
- Company 3: 10.25%
- Company 4: 24.02%
- Company 5: 59.86%

After 30 years:

- Company 1: 0.34%
- Company 2: 1.39%
- Company 3: 5.27%
- Company 4: 18.88%
- Company 5: 74.12%

After 100 years, the market is almost entirely dominated by the company with the highest profit margin:

- Company 1: 0.0016%

- Company 2: 0.171%
- Company 3: 0.136%
- Company 4: 6.58%
- Company 5: 93.26%

This mathematical model demonstrates that even small differences in profit margins can be amplified over time through compounding effects, leading to a significant concentration of market share in companies with higher margins. Over the long term, the company with the highest profit margin (Company 5) eventually dominates the entire market, while the market share of other companies dwindles to almost zero. This phenomenon reveals the essence of the "winner-takes-all" effect: even slight initial advantages can accumulate over time, ultimately leading to extreme market concentration.

1.3 Winner-Takes-All and the Advantages of Giants

The monopolistic advantages of giant companies are most evident in their control over supply chains and cost management. By deeply controlling the supply chain, they are able to procure raw materials and services at lower costs while continuously optimizing production processes to increase efficiency. This cost advantage allows giant companies to dominate in price competition, compressing profit margins and making it difficult for smaller companies to survive (Fig. 1.2).

At the same time, brand and market control further strengthen the monopolistic position of giants. Over the years, these companies have established strong brand images in the minds of consumers through continuous marketing and brand building. Brand loyalty helps these companies maintain a high market share, making it difficult for new entrants and smaller companies to break market barriers. Consumers tend to choose familiar brands, giving the giants sustained competitiveness and further reinforcing their dominant position.

In addition to their brand strength, giants possess significant technological and capital advantages that make them even more competitive compared to smaller companies. By continuously investing in technology and R&D, giant companies improve production efficiency and introduce more competitive products. These technological barriers make it

Fig. 1.2 Winners accumulate most of the resources and wealth, while smaller competitors or failures receive relatively insignificant portions

challenging for smaller companies to keep up, especially in mature industries where the innovation threshold is higher. Furthermore, giants have substantial capital reserves, enabling them to support long-term market expansion and engage in price wars, whereas smaller companies lack the capital and risk tolerance to compete.

Mechanically speaking, the reason why giants can achieve "winner-takes-all" is closely related to the compounding effect. By continually reinvesting profits into core businesses, technology upgrades, and market expansion, giants achieve sustained growth in profits. Over time, this compounding effect amplifies their market advantage, leaving smaller companies far behind in terms of profitability, gradually weakening their competitiveness.

Giant companies not only expand their market share through profit growth but also enhance their market control. As their market share increases, they can further reduce unit production costs and improve overall profit margins. This virtuous cycle leads to an ever-increasing share of industry profits going to giants, while smaller companies struggle to survive in increasingly narrow margins.

In many traditional industries, market demand and industry capacity are limited. As industries mature, market growth slows and capacity stabilizes. Giants, leveraging their advantages, quickly capture the majority of the market, leaving insufficient space for smaller companies to develop. Smaller companies not only face shrinking market share but also declining profit margins, eventually being forced out or barely surviving. As giant companies' profit margins continue to rise, the polarization of profit distribution within the industry intensifies. Giants almost entirely monopolize the primary profits of the industry, while smaller companies, even if they manage to hold a position in the market, can only obtain a small share of the profits.

1.3.1 *Case Study: Tech Giants and the Winner-Takes-All Phenomenon in the Internet Industry*

In the internet industry, tech giants such as Google, Amazon, and Facebook (Meta) have gradually monopolized industry profits through their control over platforms, technology, and data. For example, Amazon has built strong market control through its powerful logistics system, extensive product offerings, and precise user data analysis. Not only has it captured most of the online retail market, but it has also boosted overall profitability through high-margin businesses such as cloud computing. Small and medium-sized e-commerce platforms, unable to match Amazon's cost and technological advantages, are gradually pushed out or are only able to survive in niche markets. Ultimately, Amazon has achieved a "winner-takes-all" outcome in both online retail and cloud computing.

In conclusion, the "winner-takes-all" phenomenon in traditional industries stems from the ability of giant companies to gradually monopolize the market through their advantages in supply chains, brands, technology, and capital. The compounding effect further amplifies their market share and profitability, while the limited capacity of the industry exacerbates the polarization of profits, making it difficult for smaller companies to survive. This market structure not only squeezes the survival space of smaller companies but also poses challenges to the overall health of the industry. Future market regulation and policy-making need to ensure that while encouraging innovation and efficiency among giants, they also maintain fair competition in the market to prevent the negative impact of "winner-takes-all" on the industry's ecosystem.

1.4 Better to Be a Big Fish in a Small Pond: Dominating Niche Markets over Struggling in Mainstream Industries

In today's highly competitive business environment, companies often face the choice between entering a large mainstream market and leading in a niche market. Based on the earlier analysis of the "winner-takes-all" phenomenon, one key takeaway is that companies should focus on dominating niche markets rather than being a non-leading player in a large industry. Holding a dominant position in the market, especially creating a monopoly in a niche sector, can often yield higher profits. In contrast, non-leading companies in large industries face difficulties competing with industry giants due to disadvantages in resources, brand recognition, and market share (Fig. 1.3).

Niche markets typically have smaller capacities and fewer competitors, meaning that once a company takes the lead in such a market, its market share and brand recognition can rapidly grow. The high level of market concentration allows companies to leverage brand premiums and pricing strategies to achieve higher profits. For example, in high-tech and luxury sectors, leading companies often set premium prices based on their market advantages, securing extraordinary profits. The characteristics of niche markets often create higher entry barriers, including technological hurdles, brand loyalty, and specialized knowledge accumulation. For instance, Swiss luxury watch brands, although operating in a relatively small market, have established unbreakable barriers due to their craftsmanship, brand heritage, and tradition.

In niche markets, companies can focus their resources on innovation, maintaining a leading edge in technology and product offerings.

Fig. 1.3 The "Better to Be a Big Fish in a Small Pond" concept emphasizes the superior profits that companies in niche markets can achieve by leading their sector

Compared to non-leading companies in large industries, niche market leaders can respond to market changes more quickly and introduce innovative products that meet consumer demands, further solidifying their market position.

In contrast, non-leading companies in large industries often face significant challenges. Although there is substantial market demand, these industries also attract numerous competitors, particularly giant companies with vast resources. In this environment, non-leading companies often sacrifice profit margins to maintain market share, limiting their long-term growth and sometimes being pushed to the margins. Additionally, these companies often have to spread resources across multiple areas, reducing overall efficiency and innovation capacity, making it difficult to compete with industry leaders.

In large industries, market share is often highly concentrated, with leading companies controlling most of the market and brand influence. Even if non-leading companies achieve breakthroughs in some niche areas, they often struggle to expand this advantage to broader markets due to their lack of brand influence. This limitation makes it challenging for non-leading companies to optimize costs and leverage brand premiums to generate sufficient profits.

This situation offers a crucial insight: in small markets, rapidly becoming a market leader can lead to extraordinary profits. In niche markets, companies should accurately target their market, employ differentiation strategies, and ensure they build an irreplaceable advantage in specific fields. For example, Tesla, in the early stages of the electric vehicle market, targeted the high-end market and quickly became a leader in that niche. Although the market capacity was small, Tesla's high-end brand image enabled it to achieve significant profits.

Success in niche markets depends heavily on strong brand barriers. Companies need to continually build their brand and provide excellent customer service to enhance customer loyalty, ensuring that consumers in the niche market choose only their brand. This not only prevents new competitors from entering the market but also maintains the company's competitive advantage. For example, Lululemon, with its high-quality products and strong focus on the yoga market, has built substantial brand barriers, allowing it to earn extraordinary profits in the sportswear industry.

Companies in niche markets also need to maintain constant innovation to lead market trends. Continuous innovation not only satisfies the needs of existing customers but also attracts new customers, expanding market share. For example, the high-end coffee brand Nespresso has maintained its market leadership by continuously launching new coffee machines and capsule varieties, achieving high profit margins.

The "Better to Be a Big Fish in a Small Pond" strategy reflects a company's strategic choices in different market environments. In niche markets, companies can achieve extraordinary profits through market concentration, brand barriers, and continuous innovation. In contrast, non-leading companies in large industries face challenges such as resource dispersion, intense competition, and limited profit margins. Therefore, companies should choose the right markets to focus on based on their resources and market environment, positioning themselves accurately, building strong brand barriers, and continually innovating to ensure long-term competitive advantages and profitability. This strategic choice not only helps companies survive and thrive in competitive markets but also ensures their prosperity.

References

1. R. M. Grant, Contemporary Strategy Analysis: Text and Cases Edition, 10th ed. Hoboken, NJ, USA: Wiley, 2020.
2. J. Weatherston, I. Brooks, and G. Wilkinson, The International Business Environment: Challenges and Changes. Prentice Hall, 2010.
3. K. Shahzad, S. U. Bajwa, and S. A. Zia, "Competitive Strategy: Techniques for Analyzing Industries & Competitors," South Asian Journal of Management, vol. 20, no. 3, p. 194, 2013.
4. Z. Li, J. Li, J. Chen, et al., "Innovation with Chinese Characteristics: Theory and Practice," Chinese Management Studies, 2020.
5. A. Chandra and C. A. Chao, "Growth and Evolution of High-Technology Business Incubation in China," Human Systems Management, vol. 30, no. 1–2, pp. 55–69, 2011.
6. Y. Chen and Z. Lin, "Business Intelligence Capabilities and Firm Performance: A Study in China," International Journal of Information Management, vol. 57, p. 102232, 2021.
7. M. Boussebaa, "From Cultural Differences to Cultural Globalization: Towards a New Research agenda in Cross-Cultural Management Studies," Critical Perspectives on International Business, vol. 17, no. 3, pp. 381–398, 2021.
8. H. G. Cohen, "Nations and Markets," Journal of International Economic Law, vol. 23, no. 4, pp. 793–815, 2020.
9. E. Battisti, E. A. Graziano, V. Pereira, et al., "Talent Management and Firm Performance in Emerging Markets: A Systematic Literature Review and Framework," Management Decision, vol. 61, no. 9, pp. 2757–2783, 2023.
10. X. Qi, J. H. Chan, J. Hu, et al., "Motivations for Selecting Cross-Border E-commerce as a Foreign Market Entry Mode," Industrial Marketing Management, vol. 89, pp. 50–60, 2020.
11. S. Srivastava, S. Singh, and S. Dhir, "Culture and International Business Research: A Review and Research Agenda," International Business Review, vol. 29, no. 4, p. 101709, 2020.
12. Y. Mansoori and M. Lackéus, "Comparing Effectuation to Discovery-Driven Planning, Prescriptive Entrepreneurship, Business Planning, Lean Startup, and Design Thinking," Small Business Economics, vol. 54, pp. 791–818, 2020.

CHAPTER 2

The Dark Horse of New Tracks and the Life-Death Cycle

2.1 Starting with the Billion Heartbeats of Mammals

Scientists have discovered that despite the vast differences in size and lifespan among various animals, most mammals experience between 1 and 1.5 billion heartbeats over their lifetimes. This phenomenon reflects the relationship between an animal's metabolic rate and its lifespan and has become a significant observation in biology, contributing to the development of the Lifespan-Heartbeat Hypothesis. This hypothesis suggests an intrinsic link between metabolic rate and lifespan across species.

The core idea of this hypothesis is that a faster heart rate typically corresponds to a shorter lifespan. For example, the shrew, a small mammal, has an extremely rapid heart rate, ranging from 1,200 to 1,500 beats per minute, but its lifespan is usually only 1 to 2 years. In contrast, the blue whale, one of the largest animals on Earth, has a very slow heart rate of just 5 to 10 beats per minute, yet it can live for 70 to 80 years. This correlation illustrates a clear relationship between heart rate and lifespan (Fig. 2.1).

Scientists believe that the principle behind this phenomenon is related to metabolic rate. A faster heart rate signifies a higher metabolic rate, which can lead to quicker resource consumption and cellular degradation, ultimately shortening lifespan. Conversely, a slower heart rate corresponds to a lower metabolic rate, leading to slower resource consumption and

X. Cao, *Modern Business Management*,
https://doi.org/10.1007/978-981-96-0594-1_2

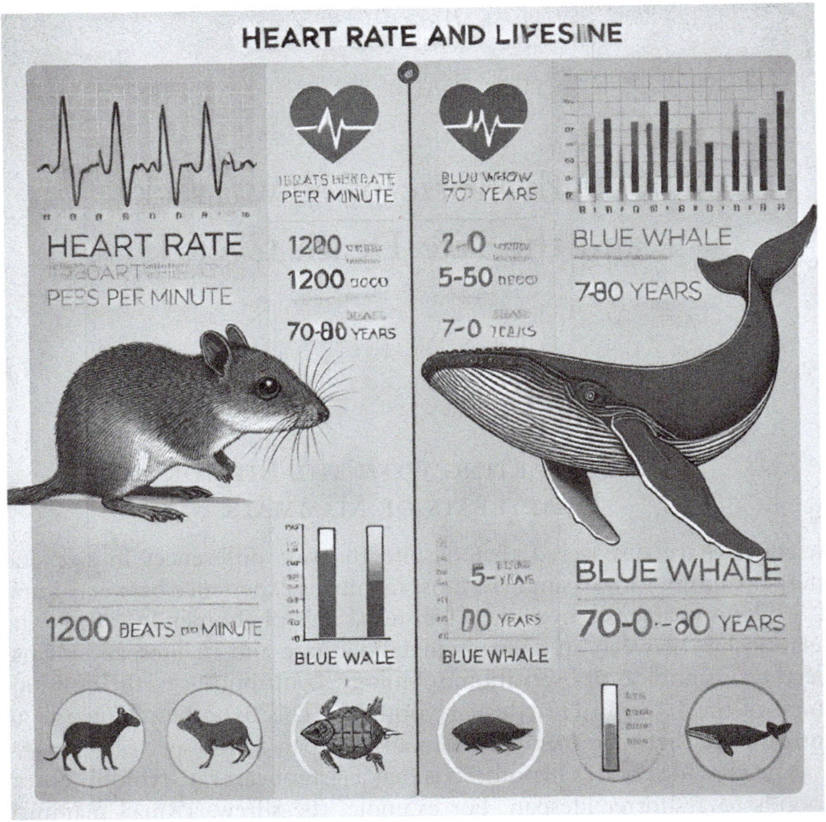

Fig. 2.1 The shrew's heart rate may reach 1,200 to 1,500 beats per minute, yet it lives only 1 to 2 years. The blue whale's heart rate is just 5 to 10 beats per minute, but it can live for 70 to 80 years. However, both species experience a similar number of total heartbeats over their lifetimes

reduced stress on cellular renewal and repair, thus extending lifespan. This relationship has been extensively validated among mammals, supporting the general applicability of the Lifespan-Heartbeat Hypothesis.

However, this hypothesis is not an absolute scientific law but rather an empirical rule. There are exceptions, such as in humans. The average heart rate for an adult human ranges between 60 and 100 beats per minute, and when calculated over an 80-year lifespan, the total number of heartbeats can approach 3 billion—far exceeding the 1 to 1.5 billion range observed in other mammals. This suggests that human lifespan is influenced by many factors beyond mere heart rate, such as advancements in medicine, technology, and social progress, which have significantly extended human life expectancy. Modern medical developments have cured or managed many diseases, while factors like social security, healthy lifestyles, and mental well-being have also played critical roles. Therefore, while the Lifespan-Heartbeat Hypothesis holds to some extent for humans, technological progress has enabled us to transcend the limits that this rule might impose.

In summary, the Lifespan-Heartbeat Hypothesis offers a valuable perspective on the relationship between lifespan and physiological activity in animals. Although it does not apply universally, particularly to humans, it reveals a general trend among mammals, particularly in wild species not influenced by human intervention. This hypothesis highlights that lifespan is not solely determined by genetics but is also closely related to metabolic and physiological processes, providing useful insights for further research into the mechanisms of life expectancy.

2.2 The Lifespan-Heartbeat Hypothesis: Implications for Us

In biology, the Lifespan-Heartbeat Hypothesis suggests that faster heart rates generally correlate with shorter lifespans. This principle, though rooted in animal physiology, also offers profound insights into the relationship between iteration speed and lifecycle in modern technology and business.

First, this principle tells us that the faster something evolves or iterates, the shorter its overall lifecycle might be. Technological advancements have significantly accelerated the development cycles of many products and services. For instance, tech products now undergo shorter development cycles, software updates happen more frequently, image resolutions have dramatically improved in a short period, and CPU processing speeds continue to break new ground. These examples show that as technology progresses, the speed of iteration increases markedly. However, this rapid iteration does not necessarily prolong the lifespan of these technologies or companies. On the contrary, just as a faster heart rate shortens an animal's life, rapid iteration often shortens the market lifecycle of tech products, as they are quickly replaced by newer generations due to intense market competition, fast-paced technological updates, and shifting consumer demands.

For example, Taobao, once considered the dominant force in e-commerce, was swiftly challenged and, in some areas, surpassed by Pinduoduo, a dark horse that rose rapidly with an innovative business model and differentiated strategy. This is a direct result of accelerated iteration driven by technological advancement. Pinduoduo's success stems not only from its business model innovation but also from its ability to align with technological trends and capitalize on shifting consumer demands in a new market segment. However, this rapid rise also intensifies market competition, increasing pressure on other platforms and potentially shortening their market lifecycles.

Looking ahead, as technology continues to evolve, the lifecycles of products and companies may become increasingly shorter. The rapid pace of technological advancement forces companies to face ever more intense competition and quicker technological iterations. In emerging markets, even today's industry giants may be replaced tomorrow by faster, more innovative competitors if they cannot keep pace with these changes. This accelerating trend may push many tech companies and products into what might be described as a "life-death cycle"—a state where they face the risk of rapid obsolescence even as they emerge (Fig. 2.2).

Therefore, the Lifespan-Heartbeat Hypothesis holds significant meaning not only in biology but also in understanding the dynamics of modern technology and business. It serves as a reminder that while rapid development and innovation are crucial, they also come with the risk of shortened lifecycles. Although technological advancement drives societal progress, it also forces companies and products to adapt quickly in a highly competitive environment, where only those capable of continuous innovation and rapid market adaptation can achieve success within their often brief lifespans.

2.3 Slowing Down to Outpace: The Wisdom of the New Era

In an era where everything seems to be accelerating, we face unprecedented challenges and opportunities. The iteration speed of new technologies and products is faster than ever, with new trends emerging almost daily. In this context, many choose to become "trend chasers,"

Fig. 2.2 Different animals have varying lifespans—turtles and whales have long lifespans, while some insects, like mayflies, live only for a few hours to a few days in their adult stages, echoing Zhuangzi's sentiment of "life and death in a single moment"

trying to stay ahead by catching every new wave. However, as iteration speeds increase, it often becomes increasingly difficult to succeed by merely following trends (Fig. 2.3).

An alternative, and potentially more sustainable, approach is to slow down and focus on deeply cultivating a specific field—especially one that may not be in the limelight but still holds substantial value. In today's fast-paced world, the value of deep cultivation is becoming more apparent.

Fig. 2.3 Focused deep work vs. trend chasing. On the left, a farmer concentrates on cultivating crops, while on the right, market chaos ensues as people constantly switch industries in blind pursuit of the next big thing

While such fields may not be popular or may even seem somewhat niche, persistence and focus can help carve out a unique position in a competitive market.

The advantage of deep cultivation lies in its independence from the volatility of external trends, instead relying on the accumulation of intrinsic value. As other areas evolve rapidly, the inherent value of deeply cultivated fields may gradually come to the fore, potentially unleashing significant potential at the right moment. History is replete with examples of technologies and industries that were initially overlooked but eventually became mainstream. Artificial intelligence and big data, for instance, were niche areas a decade ago, but today they are central to driving societal progress. As the saying goes, "Good things come to those who wait;" similarly, a deeply cultivated field of significant value will eventually gain market recognition at the right time.

In the past, when iteration speeds were slower, even if you had better technology or higher innovation, it could take a long time for the market to recognize and accept it. The promotion and realization of value for new technologies were often constrained by the slow pace of information dissemination and people's resistance to change. As a result, many potential technologies and products could not realize their value quickly due to the immaturity of the market.

However, today's era is different. The speed of information dissemination is unprecedented, and the market's willingness to accept new technologies has also improved. Once a technology or product demonstrates its value, it can spread faster than ever before. Therefore, if we can deeply cultivate and strategically position ourselves in a particular field, we will be well-placed to capitalize on opportunities when market conditions are right.

In summary, while chasing trends may be exhilarating, those who can remain patient and deeply cultivate their chosen fields are more likely to succeed in the long term. Deep cultivation not only allows us to build unique competitive advantages but also provides a solid foundation in a rapidly changing market. In future market competition, those who take the time to deeply cultivate their fields will have a better chance of leading industry development and becoming the real winners.

2.4 Persisting in Long-Termism

In many industries, true leaders are not those who blindly follow trends but those who steadfastly cultivate a specific field. While they may be overlooked in the short term by market trends, their deep accumulation and focus eventually reveal unique competitiveness and advantages at the right time. Meanwhile, those who merely chase trends, lacking depth and accumulation, are often easily eliminated by the market.

Industry leaders typically spend years cultivating a specific field, accumulating extensive experience and technology. This deep accumulation is not just a reserve of knowledge and skills; it also includes a profound understanding of industry trends and a precise grasp of market needs. Although these deep cultivators may initially face market neglect and resource constraints, their patience and persistence ultimately yield long-term rewards. For example, Apple focused on computer development in its early days, despite facing numerous competitors and market uncertainties. However, its deep cultivation in product design, user experience, and innovation eventually made it a global leader in technology (Fig. 2.4).

Fig. 2.4 Long-termism: The power of patience and accumulation. The tree grows strong and full over time, nurtured by a gardener's careful attention, from sapling to lush, mature tree

In contrast, trend chasers often enter the market quickly during the early stages of new technologies or trends but lack a deep understanding of the industry and long-term strategic planning. As market trends shift or new technologies emerge, these trend chasers, lacking sufficient depth and accumulation, quickly lose their competitive edge. For instance, many startups emerge in hot fields, but without a deep understanding of the industry and a lasting strategic vision, they are quickly overtaken by the market when new innovations appear.

Furthermore, deep cultivators accumulate not only technology and products but also a profound understanding of industry rules and market dynamics. They can anticipate and adapt to industry changes, adjust their strategies in time, and position themselves advantageously during market transitions. Companies like General Electric (GE) and Siemens, despite facing multiple market shifts and rapid technological iterations, have maintained their leading positions through long-term technological accumulation and deep industry cultivation.

The advantage of deep cultivation is that it allows companies to remain stable and resilient amidst market changes, rather than relying solely on short-term market trends. Through long-term accumulation and continuous innovation, they can build barriers to entry, establishing a competitive advantage that is difficult to replicate. This advantage extends beyond technology to brand reputation, customer relationships, and market influence.

In conclusion, the true leaders in any industry are often those who have the patience to deeply cultivate their chosen fields. While they may not be immediately recognized, their long-term accumulation and deep understanding enable them to emerge when the time is right. In contrast, trend chasers, lacking industry depth and strategic foresight, often struggle to maintain long-term competitiveness in a rapidly changing market. Therefore, in today's fast-paced world, deep cultivation and long-termism remain the keys to sustained success.

References

1. S. Collinson, R. Narula, A. Qamar, et al., International Business. Pearson UK, 2020.
2. K. Black, Business Statistics: For Contemporary Decision Making, International Adaptation. John Wiley & Sons, 2024.
3. I. Farida and D. Setiawan, "Business Strategies and Competitive Advantage:

The Role of Performance and Innovation," Journal of Open Innovation: Technology, Market, and Complexity, vol. 8, no. 3, p. 163, 2022.
4. J. Paul, "Marketing in Emerging Markets: A Review, Theoretical Synthesis and Extension," International Journal of Emerging Markets, vol. 15, no. 3, pp. 446–468, 2020.
5. S. Rana, S. Prashar, M. K. Barai, et al., "Determinants of International Marketing Strategy for Emerging Market Multinationals," International Journal of Emerging Markets, vol. 16, no. 2, pp. 154–178, 2021.
6. J. Li, G. Qian, K. Z. Zhou, et al., "Belt and Road Initiative, Globalization and Institutional Changes: Implications for Firms in Asia," Asia Pacific Journal of Management, pp. 1–14, 2022.
7. D. J. Teece, "Fundamental Issues in Strategy: Time to Reassess," Strategic Management Review, vol. 1, no. 1, pp. 103–144, 2020.
8. C. Zhang, "Formal and Informal Institutional Legacies and Inward Foreign Direct Investment into Firms: Evidence from China," Journal of International Business Studies, vol. 53, no. 6, pp. 1228–1256, 2022.
9. X. Qi, J. H. Chan, J. Hu, et al., "Motivations for Selecting Cross-Border E-commerce as a Foreign Market Entry Mode," Industrial Marketing Management, vol. 89, pp. 50–60, 2020.
10. R. W. Tang, "Pro-market Institutions and Outward FDI of Emerging Market Firms: An Institutional Arbitrage Logic," International Business Review, vol. 30, no. 3, p. 101814, 2021.

CHAPTER 3

Don't Put All Your Eggs in One Basket vs. Going All-In on a Single Venture

3.1 The Contrasting Investment Philosophies

In the world of investing, you often hear the advice, "Don't put all your eggs in one basket," which suggests diversifying your portfolio to spread risk. The core of this strategy is to minimize the impact of a single investment's failure on your overall assets. However, we also see successful investors and entrepreneurs who concentrate large amounts of capital into a single business or field they believe in strongly—sometimes even going "all-in" on their ventures. At first glance, these two approaches seem contradictory, but upon deeper analysis, each has its own logic and potential for success depending on the context (Fig. 3.1).

Diversification (Spreading Risk): This strategy aims to reduce the impact of any single investment's failure by spreading investments across various assets, industries, or regions. For example, an investor might allocate funds across stocks, bonds, real estate, and other asset classes. This method can minimize overall losses caused by fluctuations in a particular market or asset class.

Concentration (Focusing Investment): Successful investors and entrepreneurs often have deep understanding and confidence in a particular business or industry, leading them to concentrate most of their resources into the projects they believe have the greatest potential. This approach is based on thorough research, specialized knowledge, and a strong belief in future returns. Concentrated investors usually possess a

X. Cao, *Modern Business Management*,
https://doi.org/10.1007/978-981-96-0594-1_3

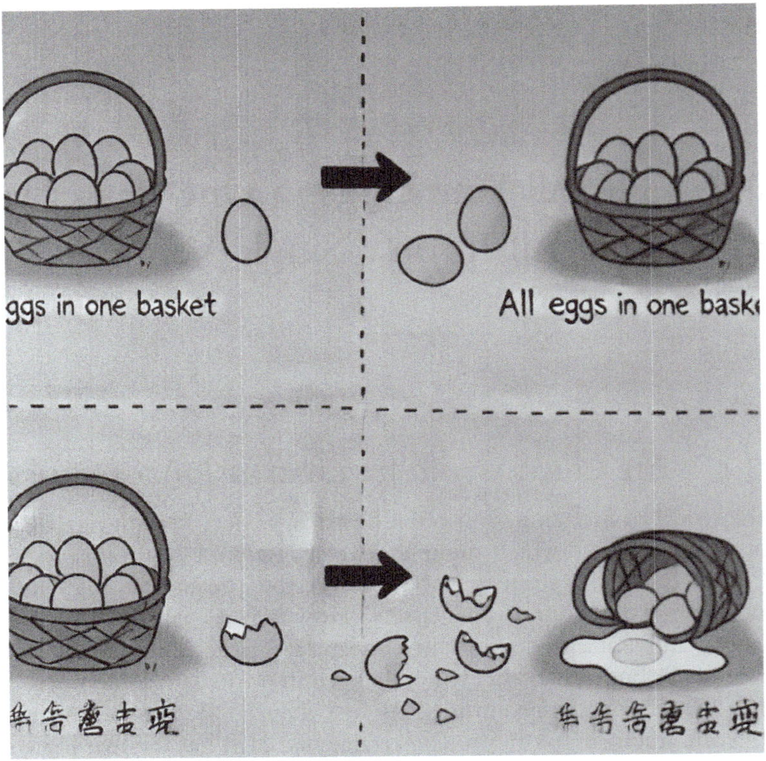

Fig. 3.1 Should you put all your eggs in one basket?

high level of expertise and market insight, allowing them to make precise decisions when assessing risks and opportunities.

The reason successful investors and entrepreneurs are able to concentrate significant resources is due to their deep understanding and high confidence in the target business or industry. This confidence typically stems from detailed research, professional knowledge, and accurate market trend predictions. For instance, some investors might heavily invest in a company they believe has a long-term competitive advantage, relying on in-depth analysis and strong trust in its business model.

Diversification and concentration can be flexibly applied at different stages or in different contexts. Early in their investment journey, investors might choose broad diversification to explore market opportunities and gain experience. However, when a particular field or company shows clear potential, they may choose to concentrate more resources on these high-potential projects. This strategy shift is usually based on continuous evaluation of market conditions and investment opportunities.

Successful entrepreneurs often commit all their energy to the businesses they founded or lead. This "all-in" attitude is driven by a strong belief in their company's vision, products, and market opportunities. Going all-in helps entrepreneurs harness their creativity and execution power, but it is typically based on a deep understanding of the market and competition. For example, famous investor Warren Buffett has made concentrated investments in companies like Coca-Cola through his firm Berkshire Hathaway. The success of this investment strategy is based on a profound understanding of Coca-Cola's long-term growth potential and strong confidence in its market position. Similarly, Steve Jobs' "all-in" approach at Apple reflects a concentrated investment strategy. He dedicated all his energy and resources to Apple's product innovation and development, leading to Apple's tremendous success despite facing significant challenges in its early days.

Diversification and concentration are not necessarily opposing strategies; they can be adjusted according to specific circumstances and the investor's expertise. For general investors, diversification is an effective way to reduce risk. However, for those with deep professional knowledge, market insight, and high confidence, concentrated investments can yield higher returns in the areas they understand well. Successful investing and entrepreneurship often involve balancing and flexibly applying these two strategies, relying on a deep understanding of the market, a reasonable assessment of risks, and accurate identification of future opportunities.

3.2 The Role of Confidence in Information and Forecasting

Whether to diversify or concentrate investments hinges on our confidence in the investment opportunity. Specifically, this confidence determines our ability to reasonably assess and predict the risks and returns of an investment.

When faced with significant uncertainty or when our knowledge of the investment target is limited, diversification is an effective risk management strategy. Diversifying investments involves spreading funds across multiple assets to reduce the impact of any single failure on the overall portfolio.

For example, if we are unsure about the details of a particular market or company, we can spread our investments across different companies or asset classes to lower overall risk.

Conversely, when we have high confidence in a particular investment and can accurately predict its future performance, concentrated investments may offer higher returns. This decision is based on a deep understanding of the market or project, enabling precise forecasts of investment returns. Concentrated investment means allocating most or all resources to an opportunity we are highly confident in, maximizing potential rewards. For instance, an entrepreneur with a clear vision for their company's future and a deep understanding of market trends might choose to invest all resources into that company, possibly achieving great success.

Consider the following example:

Imagine you are betting on where a cannonball will land. Each bet costs \$1, and you win \$10 if you guess correctly, otherwise, you lose your \$1 bet. If you know the general area where the cannonball will land but are uncertain about the exact spot, or if you lack complete information about the firing angle, speed, etc., a reasonable strategy would be to spread your bets across multiple possible landing spots. For instance, with a budget of \$100, you might place \$1 on each of 100 different positions. This strategy increases your chances of winning by diversifying your bets over a larger area (Fig. 3.2).

Now, suppose you have detailed information about the cannon's firing angle, wind speed, and trajectory, allowing you to accurately calculate where the cannonball will land. In this case, the optimal strategy would be to place all \$100 on the precise spot you calculated. With sufficient confidence in this landing point, such a bet would maximize your return.

Therefore, the core of investment decisions lies in confidence. When you have high confidence in an investment's prospects and sufficient information to support your predictions, concentrated investments can yield higher returns. Conversely, when faced with high uncertainty, diversification can help reduce risk and protect your assets. Understanding this principle allows us to make more appropriate decisions in different investment scenarios. If you have sufficient knowledge and confidence in an opportunity, concentrating resources can maximize your potential returns; if you face significant uncertainty, diversification will help manage risk more effectively.

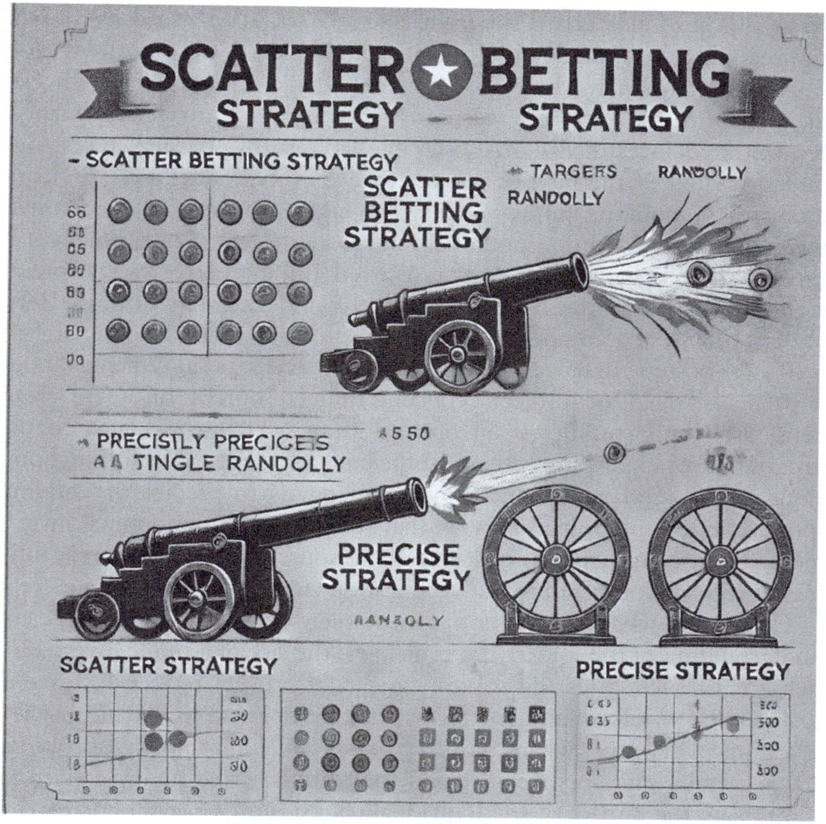

Fig. 3.2 Understanding diversification vs. concentration through predicting the landing point of a cannonball

3.3 Confidence in Information and Predictions

When faced with significant uncertainty or when we have major blind spots in our understanding of an investment, diversification is an effective strategy. By spreading resources across multiple investments, we can reduce the impact of any single failure on the overall portfolio. Diversification effectively hedges against risks arising from incomplete information or insufficient understanding. For example, in financial markets, investors often allocate funds across different asset classes, such as stocks, bonds, and real estate, to mitigate the risk of a single market's volatility.

However, when we have sufficient confidence in a particular investment opportunity and can accurately predict its future performance, concentrated investments may offer higher returns. In such cases, our understanding of the field or project exceeds the average level, and our predictions about its future success are highly accurate. Concentrated investments can maximize potential returns and leverage our professional expertise in a specific area. Just as Warren Buffett makes heavy investments in companies he believes in, such confidence stems from a deep understanding of a company's long-term value and market potential.

If we possess detailed information and accurate judgments about a particular field or project, concentrating resources on these well-considered opportunities is an optimal strategy. Referring back to the cannonball example, if we have sufficient knowledge about the firing angle, speed, and wind conditions, enabling us to predict the landing spot accurately, placing all bets on that spot is clearly the optimal investment strategy. In this case, concentrated resources will bring significantly higher returns compared to a diversification strategy.

Conversely, when information is incomplete or when we lack sufficient understanding of the underlying principles, the risk of a single investment is high. In such cases, diversification can effectively reduce losses due to incomplete information or incorrect judgments. For instance, when investing in startups, where industry prospects and company operations are uncertain, investors often spread their funds across multiple startups to mitigate the impact of any individual failure on the overall portfolio.

Steve Jobs' total commitment to Apple is a classic example. He had a clear vision and strategy for Apple's future, with a deep understanding of technology trends and market needs, leading him to concentrate all his energy and resources on Apple. Ultimately, this focused effort brought tremendous success, making Apple a global leader in the tech industry.

In financial markets, many investors adopt diversification strategies when facing emerging markets or high uncertainty. For instance, investment funds often spread their money across various stocks and bonds to cope with market fluctuations and risks. This approach effectively avoids significant losses caused by the failure of a single investment.

Confidence plays a crucial role in determining investment strategy. When you have high confidence in a particular field or project, and sufficient information, concentrated investments often yield higher returns.

However, when faced with uncertainty or incomplete information, diversification is a more prudent choice. Successful investors typically adjust their strategies based on their understanding of the market and investment opportunities, maximizing returns while effectively managing risk. Thus, understanding and applying this principle helps investors make wiser decisions in different contexts. Whether to concentrate or diversify investments depends on information mastery and future predictions.

3.4 Don't Earn Beyond Your Knowledge

Concentrated investment involves allocating most of your funds into one or a few investment opportunities. When investors have high confidence and deep understanding of these opportunities, this strategy can fully leverage their knowledge and forecasting abilities in a specific field, potentially achieving higher returns. Concentrated investment allows investors to maximize their commitment to promising investment targets, using their deep market understanding to capture excess returns.

Compared to diversification, concentrated investments typically yield higher profits because they avoid diluting returns. Diversification spreads funds across multiple assets to reduce the risk of any single investment failing, but this also dilutes returns, potentially leading to lower overall gains. Concentrated investments allow investors to focus all their energy and resources on high-confidence opportunities, pursuing higher returns, albeit with higher risks.

The phrase "Don't earn beyond your knowledge" emphasizes the importance of personal knowledge and expertise in making investment decisions. Investors who operate within their areas of expertise can make more accurate judgments and forecasts, effectively seizing investment opportunities. When investors deeply understand an industry or company, they can better assess its potential and risks, choosing to concentrate investments in these high-confidence opportunities.

Expertise and knowledge can significantly improve the quality of investment decisions. Investors specializing in a field can leverage their deep understanding of the market, technology, or companies to make more informed investment decisions. For example, an investor specializing in the tech sector who deeply understands AI trends might choose to concentrate investments in innovative AI companies, confident in the field's future growth.

On the other hand, some investors may choose to diversify in fields they are less familiar with to reduce overall risk. For example, a general investor might spread investments across various stocks and bonds, recognizing that while returns might not be exceptionally high, this approach effectively reduces the impact of any single investment failure on their overall assets.

When investors conduct deep research in a field and have high confidence in their investment targets, concentrated investment can yield higher returns by avoiding dilution. Simultaneously, this strategy requires investors to have sufficient knowledge and expertise to manage risk effectively. In situations with high uncertainty, diversification remains a more prudent strategy, though it may sacrifice some potential returns.

3.5 Achieving High Returns with Low Risk

In investing, many emphasize the importance of diversification to reduce risk. However, diversification is not suitable for all investors, especially those with deep industry knowledge and experience. For these investors, focusing on familiar and specialized fields not only allows them to better manage risk but also achieve high returns (Fig. 3.3).

Firstly, the essence of investing lies in balancing risk and return, which is based on the investor's ability to recognize and manage risk. When investors enter familiar fields, they have keen insights into industry trends, market changes, and potential risks. This knowledge advantage enables them to assess investment opportunities more accurately and maximize returns while keeping risks under control. Conversely, if they diversify into unfamiliar fields, they might dilute some risks but, due to a lack of deep understanding, may struggle to make the right decisions, potentially leading to unexpected losses.

Secondly, focusing on familiar areas allows investors to concentrate their efforts, avoiding the resource waste that can come from diversification. With limited time and energy, investors cannot master every field. Therefore, trying to diversify across multiple areas often results in inadequate expertise in any of them, making it challenging to identify and seize high-return opportunities. On the other hand, focusing on one's strengths enables investors to better grasp market dynamics and make quick, accurate decisions, which is crucial for achieving high returns.

Moreover, concentrating investments in familiar areas gives investors more confidence in facing market fluctuations and sudden risks. Because

Fig. 3.3 Risk and return often appear contradictory. However, in familiar fields, it is possible to achieve low risk and high returns

they deeply understand the field's underlying logic, market rules, and competitive environment, they can remain calm and make rational decisions even during short-term market volatility. This confidence stems from a profound understanding of their expertise, significantly reducing the uncontrollability of risks.

In conclusion, achieving high returns with low risk hinges on focusing investments within one's knowledge and expertise. While diversification may seem to lower risk, it often dilutes returns and increases exposure to unknown risks. Only by thoroughly understanding and controlling risk can investors concentrate investments in familiar fields, achieving high returns while maintaining relatively low risk. Investors should remember that making money within their knowledge domain is the key to long-term profitability.

References

1. J. Baylis, J. J. Wirtz, and J. L. Johnson, Eds., Strategy in the Contemporary World. Oxford University Press, 2022.
2. A. Johnsen, "Strategic Planning in Turbulent Times: Still Useful?" Public Policy and Administration, vol. 38, no. 4, pp. 445–465, 2023.
3. I. K. Arslan, "The Importance of Creating Customer Loyalty in Achieving Sustainable Competitive Advantage," Eurasian Journal of Business and Management, vol. 8, no. 1, pp. 11–20, 2020.
4. G. Fuertes, M. Alfaro, M. Vargas, et al., "Conceptual Framework for the Strategic Management: A Literature Review—Descriptive," Journal of Engineering, vol. 2020, no. 1, p. 6253013, 2020.
5. C. L. Pedersen, T. Ritter, and C. A. Di Benedetto, "Managing Through a Crisis: Managerial Implications for Business-to-Business Firms," Industrial Marketing Management, vol. 88, pp. 314–322, 2020.
6. C. Katsikeas, L. Leonidou, and A. Zeriti, "Revisiting International Marketing Strategy in a Digital Era: Opportunities, Challenges, and Research Directions," International Marketing Review, vol. 37, no. 3, pp. 405–424, 2020.
7. L. Argote, S. Lee, and J. Park, "Organizational Learning Processes and Outcomes: Major Findings and Future Research Directions," Management Science, vol. 67, no. 9, pp. 5399–5429, 2021.
8. A. Tawse and P. Tabesh, "Thirty Years with the Balanced Scorecard: What We Have Learned," Business Horizons, vol. 66, no. 1, pp. 123–132, 2023.
9. P. Amason and A. Ward, Strategic Management: From Theory to Practice. Routledge, 2020.
10. F. Luthans, B. C. Luthans, and K. W. Luthans, Organizational Behavior: An Evidence-Based Approach, 14th ed. IAP, 2021.

CHAPTER 4

Top-Down Management vs. Bottom-Up Innovation

4.1 KPI vs. OKR

In modern corporate management, KPIs (Key Performance Indicators) and OKRs (Objectives and Key Results) are two widely used performance management tools. KPIs are closely tied to an organization's strategic objectives, emphasizing specific, quantifiable outcomes. For instance, sales figures, profit margins, and customer satisfaction can all be used as KPIs. A key characteristic of KPIs is their focus on controlling processes and achieving results aligned with the company's business objectives. In contrast, OKR is a goal-oriented management tool that includes clear objectives (Objectives) and measurable key results (Key Results) that assess progress toward these objectives. OKR goals are often challenging and ambitious, not necessarily achievable with ease (Fig. 4.1).

While both aim to improve overall corporate performance, they differ significantly in philosophy, implementation, and application scenarios. Take the example of a mature mechanical industry. In such industries, production processes are usually very stable and standardized. We can precisely estimate the time and cost required to produce a wheel axle, and there are clear standards for controlling defect rates. In such cases, companies can easily measure employee performance by setting KPIs, as each metric is specific and quantifiable, directly corresponding to the expected outcomes of the business.

X. Cao, *Modern Business Management*,
https://doi.org/10.1007/978-981-96-0594-1_4

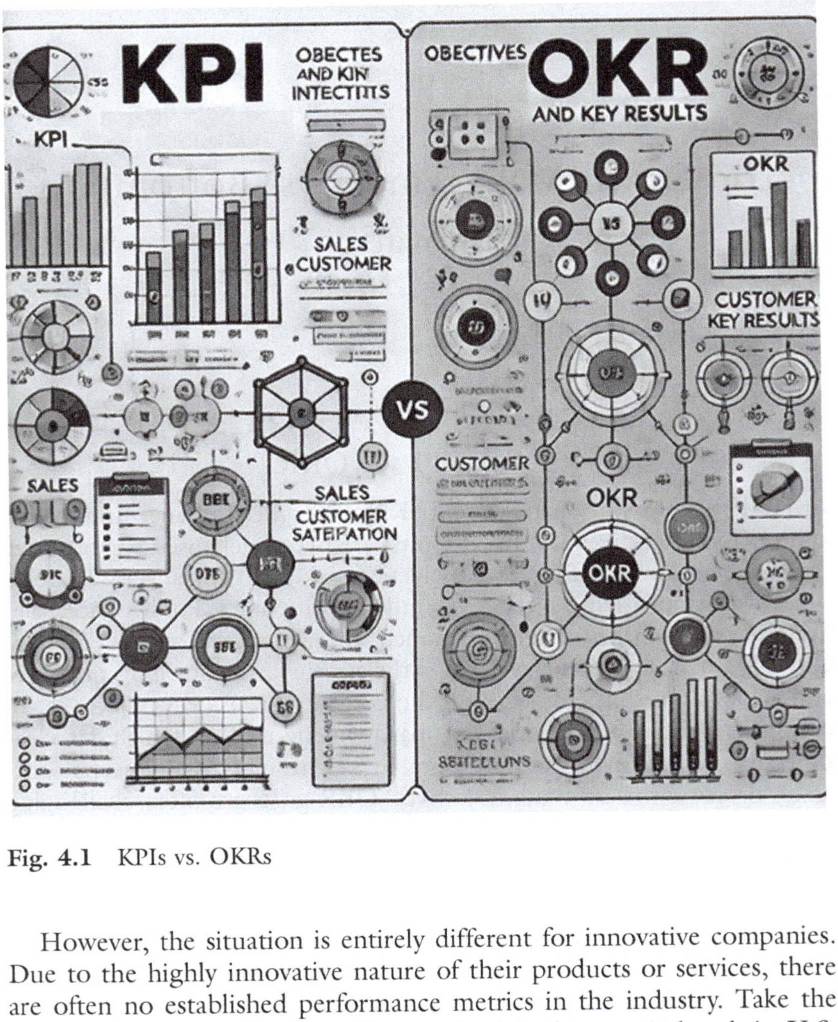

Fig. 4.1 KPIs vs. OKRs

However, the situation is entirely different for innovative companies. Due to the highly innovative nature of their products or services, there are often no established performance metrics in the industry. Take the Manhattan Project, the first effort to develop the atomic bomb in U.S. history, as an example. This mission was full of exploration and unknowns, making it difficult to assess the researchers involved through precise quantitative indicators. For tasks filled with uncertainty and challenges, KPIs, which emphasize specific metrics, are difficult to apply effectively since outcomes and processes cannot be measured by fixed standards. In this context, the flexibility and goal orientation of OKR make it more suitable. OKR encourages setting challenging goals and allows for adjustments during implementation based on actual conditions. This approach not only motivates employees to innovate and push boundaries but also better adapts to the uncertainties inherent in research and development tasks. Therefore, OKR is more suitable than KPI for measuring and driving performance improvement in innovative companies, particularly in environments characterized by exploration and unknowns.

Typically, KPI assessments are periodic, possibly conducted monthly, quarterly, or annually, with relatively stable targets. Additionally, KPIs are usually set top-down, determined by senior management and then cascaded down to departments and employees. Compared to KPI, OKR emphasizes flexibility. It often involves setting challenging goals over shorter cycles, such as quarterly, with the ability to adjust these goals as circumstances change. Another significant feature of OKR is its transparency and collaborative nature, often made public company-wide to foster cross-departmental collaboration and communication. Moreover, the OKR setting process is often bottom-up, with more employee and team participation rather than top-down assignments.

Although KPI and OKR differ in many ways, their purpose is the same: to help companies achieve strategic goals and improve organizational performance. Both rely on specific metrics to evaluate employee performance and are essential tools for performance evaluation, influencing employee rewards and promotions.

Specifically, KPIs focus more on ensuring that employees complete predefined tasks and goals, emphasizing the assessment of past performance. The goals are typically assigned by superiors and remain fixed, making KPIs suitable for environments with stable business processes. On the other hand, OKRs focus on future challenges and innovation, encouraging employees to exceed existing goals. OKR targets are more flexible, giving employees a greater sense of participation and making it more suitable for rapidly changing environments. OKRs are particularly common in internet companies or in innovation-driven departments such as Research and Development (R&D) and marketing, where frequent goal adjustments and a focus on innovation are crucial.

In summary, both KPI and OKR have their strengths and weaknesses. KPIs are ideal for business scenarios requiring stable execution, while OKRs are better suited to environments that demand rapid responses to change, encourage innovation, and foster team collaboration. In practice, many modern companies use a combination of KPI and OKR, selecting the most appropriate management tool based on specific circumstances to maximize organizational effectiveness.

4.2 Military-Style Management vs. the Emergence of Innovation

KPI and OKR are two distinct performance management tools with significant differences in management structure and task execution. KPI is typically suited to top-down management models, while OKR is better suited to bottom-up management approaches. These methods have their respective advantages and applicability in different work scenarios.

The top-down management model reflected in KPI aligns with traditional management concepts, especially in scenarios where processes are highly standardized, and tasks are highly predictable. Management first develops an overall plan and objectives, which are then broken down into departmental and individual KPIs. Employees guide their work based on these KPIs, ensuring that the entire organization is working toward a common direction. This military-style management approach clearly defines employees' work content, time allocation, and expected outcomes, effectively controlling the entire process and minimizing deviations. This method is particularly effective in manufacturing, supply chain management, and administrative tasks, where work content is relatively fixed and predictable, making it easy to set clear performance standards and timelines.

However, when dealing with tasks full of uncertainty, the limitations of KPIs become apparent. When tasks require a high degree of innovation and are filled with uncertainty, it is difficult to set precise goals and measure progress using traditional KPIs. For example, the uncertainty and complexity involved in scientific research projects, new product development, or market expansion make it challenging to predetermine the exact implementation path. In such cases, enforcing KPIs may not only stifle creativity but also lead to unreasonable goal setting that cannot address the continuously evolving challenges.

In contrast, OKR's bottom-up management model is better suited for handling tasks with high levels of uncertainty. OKR goals are typically proposed proactively by teams and individuals, with management providing directional guidance but not imposing strict limitations on the specific paths, time, and resources required. OKR emphasizes motivating employees to use their initiative within the goal framework, encouraging innovation and independent decision-making. This flexibility allows employees to adjust their work plans based on actual situations and explore different solutions, thereby better addressing complex problems.

For example, in technology companies, the product development process is often fraught with uncertainty. It is challenging for management to accurately estimate the time and resources required for each development stage from the outset. Through OKR, teams can set a challenging goal and independently decide how to achieve it, continuously adjusting key results as the project progresses. This method not only fosters team creativity but also allows for timely strategic adjustments based on project progress, leading to better achievement of the final goal. Drawing on Teece's Dynamic Capabilities theory, the ability to integrate, build, and reconfigure internal competencies to address rapidly changing environments becomes critical. This theory supports the argument for a flexible, innovation-driven approach in markets where rapid technological change occurs.

In summary, KPI and OKR each have advantages in different management scenarios. KPIs are suited to work environments where tasks are well-defined and processes are fixed, where top-down management ensures efficient achievement of goals. On the other hand, OKR excels in environments that require innovation and flexible responses, as the bottom-up management model provides employees with more autonomy and creative space, enabling organizations to tackle complex challenges and drive innovative outcomes. The combination of both can help companies maximize performance across different task environments.

4.3 Autocratic Management with KPI vs. Democratic Management with OKR

The management style of KPI is akin to governance in an autocratic state. In this model, instructions are passed down from the highest level of management through various tiers to each department and employee. When setting KPIs, management breaks down the company's strategic goals into detailed objectives and assigns them to employees at every level. The task of the lower-level employees is to strictly adhere to these indicators and complete the tasks assigned by their superiors. This method emphasizes obedience and execution, with employee autonomy strictly limited—they are more executors than decision-makers. This management style is suitable for tasks with high predictability, such as standardized operations on a production line or the regulated execution of administrative tasks. In such scenarios, clear instructions and precise execution ensure that tasks are efficiently completed without deviation.

In contrast, OKR resembles the management style of a democratic society. In this model, the setting of assessment indicators is more flexible. Management provides directional guidance, but the specifics of how to achieve the goals, including the time and effort required, are determined by teams and individuals. OKR encourages employees to participate in the goal-setting process and grants them enough freedom to explore and innovate. Under this approach, employees are not only executors but also decision-makers, able to adjust their work methods based on actual circumstances and actively seek optimal solutions. OKR's flexibility and autonomy can inspire employee creativity and initiative, allowing them to play a greater role in achieving goals.

This analogy also helps us understand why KPI and OKR are suited to different work environments. KPI is highly effective in tasks requiring strict control and precise execution because its autocratic nature ensures orderly and efficient task completion. Meanwhile, OKR is more appropriate for work environments with significant uncertainty and innovation demands. Through a management style akin to a democratic society, OKR can unlock employee potential, driving innovation and progress.

4.4 Choosing the Right Metrics at Different Stages of Development

Selecting the appropriate performance management tools is critical as companies go through different stages of their business lifecycle. OKR and KPI each showcase their strengths during the R&D and product phases, respectively.

When a company is in the R&D phase, adopting OKR is particularly suitable. The R&D phase is typically characterized by uncertainty and the need for innovation, where the challenges lie in exploring unknown territories, developing new technologies, or creating new products. Here, the greatest advantage of OKR is its ability to inspire innovation. By setting challenging objectives and flexible key results, OKR encourages employees to think outside the box and explore new methods and ideas. It provides teams and individuals with enough freedom to adjust strategies based on real-time conditions, enabling them to find the most effective solutions to complex problems. As a result, OKR can help R&D teams maintain momentum in uncertain environments, ignite creativity, and drive breakthrough progress in projects.

However, when a company enters the product phase or operates within product departments, KPI becomes more appropriate. During the product phase, the company usually has developed relatively mature products, and the focus shifts from innovation to optimization and scaling production. At this stage, improving efficiency becomes the key task. KPIs are characterized by setting clear, quantifiable performance metrics and strictly adhering to them. This approach ensures that teams focus on achieving objectives, optimizing production processes, controlling costs, and improving market responsiveness. KPIs can help companies achieve efficient production and market expansion, ensuring competitiveness in mature markets.

Of course, while KPIs effectively enhance efficiency in the product phase, they inevitably stifle some innovation. KPIs emphasize standardization and process control, which may limit creative thinking. However, this loss of innovation is often acceptable in the product phase, as the product has matured, and the company's expectations for innovation are relatively low. Compared to the R&D phase, the company is more concerned with optimizing operations, expanding market share, and increasing profit margins based on existing products.

4.5 Does My Company Also Need to Learn from IBM's Management Model?

IBM, a technology company renowned for its innovation-driven approach, has long been regarded as a model for many companies in its management practices. IBM's management structure incorporates a flexible evaluation method similar to OKR, which has played a vital role in inspiring employee enthusiasm for innovation and driving technological breakthroughs. By setting challenging objectives and granting employees greater freedom, IBM has maintained its leadership position in the highly competitive tech sector. This mechanism not only allows employees to explore new ideas in uncertain environments but also encourages them to break the mold, resulting in continuous innovation for the company.

However, this flexible management mechanism is not suitable for all enterprises, especially those primarily focused on efficiency and operating in mature product environments. For instance, Foxconn, a globally renowned manufacturing company, operates highly standardized production processes with stringent efficiency requirements. In such an environment, a more autocratic management model might be more appropriate. Foxconn's management approach resembles the KPI model, setting clear objectives and tasks from the top down, with employees primarily responsible for strict execution. This method ensures efficient and precise production processes, minimizing variation and uncertainty in production. For companies like Foxconn, where products are mature and innovation space is limited, optimizing processes and controlling costs become the top priorities. In this context, a management model similar to KPI, with its clear metrics and strict execution, can help maximize production efficiency and maintain cost advantages in a highly competitive market. Conversely, a more flexible OKR mechanism might lead to unclear goals and insufficient execution in such companies, potentially affecting overall efficiency.

Therefore, different enterprises need to choose the most suitable management model based on their business nature and stage of development. Innovation-driven companies like IBM can maintain technological leadership and innovation vitality by adopting management mechanisms similar to OKR. For manufacturing enterprises like Foxconn, a management model that emphasizes standardization and efficient execution is better suited to meeting their requirements for efficiency and cost control. This also illustrates that there is no one-size-fits-all standard in corporate management; rather, it should be flexibly adjusted based on the specific circumstances of the enterprise.

In corporate management, many people fall into the trap of blindly emulating the management models of rapidly developing, successful companies. However, effective management strategies are not simply about copying others' practices. Instead, they require a deep understanding of one's positioning, a clear analysis of the company's development stage, and consideration of the characteristics of different departments, leading to the adoption of the most appropriate management model.

Every enterprise has its unique business environment, market positioning, and development stage. For example, startups are typically in a stage of exploration and innovation, where flexibility and creativity are key to success. Such companies might borrow management models from innovation-driven companies like Google or IBM, adopting OKR-like mechanisms that encourage employees to explore and experiment in uncertain environments. This model can help startups find breakthroughs in competitive markets, driving innovation and growth.

However, when a company reaches a more mature stage, where the products have stabilized and the market is well-established, efficiency and execution often become more critical. In such cases, the KPI management model used by manufacturing companies like Foxconn might be more appropriate. This model ensures the efficient operation of production processes and cost control through top-down target setting and strict performance evaluation. At this point, blindly adopting the flexible management models of innovation-driven companies might backfire, leading to unclear goals, resource waste, and inefficiency.

Additionally, the functions and nature of different departments also require the adoption of different management models. R&D departments need more freedom for innovation, making them more suited to OKR. In contrast, sales or production departments benefit from clear metrics and strict management to improve performance and control quality. Therefore, when formulating management strategies, companies should fully consider the characteristics of each department and choose the most suitable management tools and methods.

In conclusion, the best management model is not a fixed template for success but one that is tailored to the specific characteristics, development stage, and departmental needs of the enterprise. Only by doing so can companies maximize their potential and ensure success in various market environments.

References

1. A. Distanont, "The Role of Innovation in Creating a Competitive Advantage," Kasetsart Journal of Social Sciences, vol. 41, no. 1, pp. 15–21, 2020.
2. G. Fuertes, M. Alfaro, M. Vargas, et al., "Conceptual Framework for the Strategic Management: A Literature Review—Descriptive," Journal of Engineering, vol. 2020, no. 1, p. 6253013, 2020.
3. R. W. Griffin, J. M. Phillips, and S. M. Gully, Organizational Behavior: Managing People and Organizations, CENGAGE Learning, 2020.
4. A. Henry, Understanding Strategic Management, Oxford University Press, 2021.

5. J. Johnson, R. Whittington, P. Regnér, et al., Exploring Strategy, Pearson UK, 2020.
6. M. J. Leiblein, J. J. Reuer, M. M. Larsen, et al., "When Are Global Decisions Strategic?," Global Strategy Journal, vol. 12, no. 4, pp. 714–737, 2022.
7. C. L. Pedersen, T. Ritter, and C. A. Di Benedetto, "Managing Through a Crisis: Managerial Implications for Business-to-Business Firms," Industrial Marketing Management, vol. 88, pp. 314–322, 2020.
8. L. Argote, S. Lee, and J. Park, "Organizational Learning Processes and Outcomes: Major Findings and Future Research Directions," Management Science, vol. 67, no. 9, pp. 5399–5429, 2021.

CHAPTER 5

Efficient Traditional Industries vs. Inefficient Emerging Industries

5.1 The "Efficiency" Behind Tech Giants: High Barriers and Excess Profits

In modern corporate management and market competition, it is commonly believed that large tech companies like IBM, Amazon, Nvidia, and Microsoft can maintain their dominant positions in highly competitive markets due to their exceptional management systems and efficient operations. This perspective seems reasonable, given that in a rapidly evolving industry, strong management is often seen as the key to a company's success. However, if we look from another angle, this assumption is not entirely accurate.

The success of these tech giants in the market is indeed partly due to their management systems, but more importantly, it is tied to the nature of the industries they operate in. First, these companies are involved in industries with high technical barriers that are difficult to replicate in the short term, such as artificial intelligence, cloud computing, and high-performance computing hardware. These fields require significant upfront investment and highly specialized knowledge and skills, which means few competitors can enter the market, allowing these companies to enjoy excess profits for an extended period.

Take Nvidia as an example. The company had been deeply involved in GPU (graphics processing unit) research and development long before the rise of artificial intelligence. When the demand for AI technology

X. Cao, *Modern Business Management*,
https://doi.org/10.1007/978-981-96-0594-1_5

surged, Nvidia, with its advantage in parallel computing through GPUs, quickly became a leader in the AI field. This industry characteristic allowed Nvidia to rapidly secure excess profits and dominate the market.

According to Nvidia's financial report, its annual revenue reached $26.4 billion in 2023, representing a year-on-year growth of over 50%. Such a profit margin is almost unimaginable in traditional manufacturing, but the industry characteristics and technical barriers in which Nvidia operates enabled it to achieve such high growth in a short period. While this high revenue reflects Nvidia's success as a company, this success is more attributed to its industry characteristics and technical barriers rather than any unique advantages in efficiency or management.

5.2 The Efficiency Kings of Traditional Industries: Intensification and Competitive Compression

Unlike high-tech companies, traditional manufacturing industries have experienced decades, if not centuries, of development, leading to intense market competition. Due to the lower entry barriers, many participants vie for market share, forcing companies to continuously improve efficiency, reduce costs, and even implement large-scale automation to lower labor costs. Ultimately, these industries enter a state of "intensification," where companies maintain survival by relentless competition over supply chain control and profit compression.

Take the Chinese home appliance manufacturing industry, one of the most competitive manufacturing sectors globally, as an example. Over the past few decades, numerous companies such as Midea, Gree, and Haier have emerged. These companies have gradually captured the global market through extreme supply chain management, large-scale production, and low-cost operations. According to statistics, China's home appliance industry held over 30% of the global market share in 2022, ranking first in the world. Although these companies' profit margins are much lower than those of tech giants, they remain competitive through efficient management and extreme cost control. While their businesses may seem low-end, their high operational efficiency is the result of years of intense competition. The success of manufacturing relies more on management and execution efficiency rather than on technological innovation and market exclusivity, as seen in tech giants.

5.3 Market Opportunities from Corporate Management: The Battle Between High-Barrier and Low-Barrier Industries

From the analysis above, we can draw an important conclusion: industries with high barriers that are difficult to replicate often enjoy excess profits for a long time, and the success of companies in these industries largely depends on industry characteristics rather than purely on management efficiency. In contrast, traditional industries, after years of development, may not have high profit margins, but companies have achieved extremely high management efficiency and cost control through continuous intensification and optimization.

This gives us an important insight: when selecting market opportunities, one must consider industry characteristics and competitive dynamics. In industries with high barriers and technical requirements, companies may gain excess profits through technological innovation and market leadership. In contrast, in industries with low entry barriers and intense competition, a company's success depends more on management efficiency and cost control.

On the surface, companies like IBM, Amazon, Nvidia, and Microsoft seem to symbolize efficiency, but their success is more supported by market positioning and technical barriers. Conversely, traditional manufacturing industries that appear low-end have, through years of intensification and competition, become the true kings of efficiency. When choosing a development direction, companies need to deeply understand the nature of the industry, considering not only the prospects of technology and the market but also assessing their management and operational capabilities to maintain a competitive edge in the fierce market.

5.4 Why Big Companies Can Tolerate Inefficiency and Even Overstaffing

High profits give companies in high-barrier, innovative industries enough financial resources to tolerate lower operational efficiency. In such cases, companies may not be in a hurry to cut costs or optimize human resources because they can sustain high levels of overstaffing through existing excess profits. Many companies in emerging industries are in the stages of research and development and technological exploration, requiring a flexible reserve of technical personnel to respond to ever-changing technological needs and market opportunities. Maintaining overstaffing can provide companies with sufficient technical strength to ensure rapid response and adjustment at critical moments.

The businesses and products of emerging companies are still in the exploratory and adjustment stages. This uncertainty means they may need more technical personnel to experiment with different solutions, develop new features, or improve existing products. Overstaffing, in this case, is not just a resource reserve but also a response to R&D needs. Companies whose businesses are not yet fully mature may not have stable operational models or efficiency optimization strategies, so they have a higher tolerance for flexibility in staffing and overstaffing. This leads to many innovative companies becoming "high-pay, low-stress" dream employers. In contrast, due to generally low-profit margins in their industries, workers on assembly lines in traditional manufacturing and cashiers in retail often work full-time under heavy workloads.

Companies in high-barrier industries, due to technical complexity and market uncertainty, usually take longer to mature and optimize. During this process, they may prioritize technological breakthroughs and market opportunities over immediate operational efficiency improvements. Therefore, these companies may appear relatively inefficient in management. For them, technological innovation and market capture are often higher priorities, while improving management efficiency and reducing costs may be delayed.

High-profit emerging companies often choose to maintain overstaffing to have sufficient technical reserves for R&D and business exploration. This choice may lead to relative inefficiency in the short term, but it provides the necessary flexibility and advantages for companies in technology and market competition. As their business gradually matures and market competition intensifies, these companies may gradually optimize efficiency and control costs to adapt to the new market environment.

5.5 The Three Stages of Industry Development

To understand the development trajectory of an industry, we can divide it into three main stages: the R&D-driven stage, the intensification stage, and the market leader stage. Each stage has its characteristics and market dynamics, which together shape the maturation process of an industry.

R&D-Driven Stage: When an industry is just emerging, the technical barriers are typically very high. At this time, only companies with core technologies can enter the market. These companies are usually recognized as high-tech enterprises in the early stages, enjoying excess profits due to industry barriers. For example, in the early days of the semiconductor and internet industries, only technology leaders like Intel and Amazon could secure significant profits thanks to their technological advantages.

Due to the presence of excess profits, companies at this stage are relatively less concerned with operational efficiency. The profits are sufficient to cover relatively inefficient operations, allowing companies to focus on R&D. For example, when artificial intelligence was just beginning, companies like Nvidia concentrated on technological innovation rather than immediately optimizing costs or improving management efficiency. High profits provided them with enough buffer space to focus on driving technological progress and market promotion rather than rushing to improve operational efficiency.

Intensification Stage: Over time, the spread of technology allows more companies to enter the field. As the technical barriers gradually lower, market competition intensifies. This stage is often accompanied by the onset of price wars, leading to the gradual erosion of excess profits. For instance, in the rapid development of the smartphone market, as technology spread and the market became saturated, more and more manufacturers joined the competition, leading to increasingly severe price wars.

In such circumstances, companies must seek new competitive advantages. As technological breakthroughs and innovations become more challenging, companies shift their focus to improving management efficiency and reducing costs. Companies enhance competitiveness by cutting supply chain costs, optimizing production processes, and lowering labor costs. Companies like Midea and Gree in China's home appliance manufacturing industry have successfully carved out a place in the global market through efficient supply chain management and large-scale production, continuously reducing costs.

Market Leader Stage: After a long period of fierce competition, industry profit margins are further compressed. Constant price wars lead to a market where only companies capable of withstanding the lowest product prices can survive. Eventually, industry consolidation results in an oligopolistic market dominated by a few, or even a single, market leader.

At this stage, surviving companies often reach an understanding to avoid reigniting price wars, maintaining relative stability and profit margins within the industry. For example, the airline and steel industries, after years of price wars and competition, have formed market structures dominated by a few large companies. These companies, following industry consolidation, typically maintain a certain level of profitability and avoid excessive competition to ensure the industry's healthy development.

In the R&D-driven stage, companies leverage technological advantages to gain excess profits, paying less attention to efficiency. In the intensification stage, as technical barriers lower and competition intensifies, companies compete for market share through management optimization and cost reduction. In the market leader stage, after intense price wars, the industry consolidates, ultimately forming a market structure dominated by the most cost-efficient companies. This process reveals the dynamic evolution of industries, showing how technological innovation, market competition, and corporate strategy influence industry structure and corporate behavior at each stage (Fig. 5.1).

5.6 Choosing the Right Time to Enter

When deciding when to enter an industry, a company's core competencies should align with the current stage of industry development to achieve the best strategic outcomes.

In the R&D-driven stage, the industry is just starting, with high technical barriers. Only companies with strong R&D capabilities or those that have already made significant early investments in the field can enter the market and gain excess profits. At this time, technological innovation is key, and improving efficiency is not the primary task. If your team excels in R&D, entering during this stage is most appropriate. For example, Nvidia secured market leadership in the early days of artificial intelligence through its powerful GPU technology.

As technology becomes widespread and market competition intensifies, the intensification stage becomes critical. In this stage, technical barriers lower, price wars become frequent, and companies must maintain competitiveness through cost optimization and management efficiency. At this point, companies with strong intensification capabilities, such as excellent supply chain management and cost control, will stand out. If your team is skilled at reducing costs and improving efficiency, entering during the

Fig. 5.1 Industry development includes three stages: R&D-driven stage, intensification stage, market leader stage

intensification stage is a wiser choice. For example, Chinese home appliance manufacturers Midea and Gree succeeded in a highly competitive market through efficient production and management strategies.

After long-term competition, the market eventually becomes dominated by a few or even one leading company. These companies maintain stable profit margins through low-cost strategies and market consolidation. At this stage, unless you have been deeply involved in the industry for many years, it is unwise to blindly enter an industry that has already been monopolized by a market leader.

In summary, companies should choose the optimal entry timing based on their core competencies: companies with strong R&D capabilities should enter during the R&D-driven stage; companies with intensification capabilities should enter during the intensification stage; it is not advisable to enter an industry already in the market leader stage unless you are the market leader with years of deep involvement in that industry.

References

1. S. S. A. Shah and Z. Khan, "Corporate Social Responsibility: A Pathway to Sustainable Competitive Advantage?," International Journal of Bank Marketing, vol. 38, no. 1, pp. 159–174, 2020.
2. P. Pananond, G. Gereffi, and T. Pedersen, "An Integrative Typology of Global Strategy and Global Value Chains: The Management and Organization of Cross-Border Activities," Global Strategy Journal, vol. 10, no. 3, pp. 421–443, 2020.
3. S. Aujirpongpan and Y. Hareebin, "The Effect of Strategic Intuition, Business Analytics, Networking Capabilities, and Dynamic Strategy on Innovation Performance: The Empirical Study Thai Processed Food Exporters," The Journal of Asian Finance, Economics and Business, vol. 7, no. 1, pp. 259–268, 2020.
4. P. Sharma, T. Y. Leung, R. P. J. Kingshott, et al., "Managing Uncertainty During a Global Pandemic: An International Business Perspective," Journal of Business Research, vol. 116, pp. 188–192, 2020.
5. M. Sirfraz, "Corporate Strategy Formulation: A Theoretical Review."
6. L. Argote, S. Lee, and J. Park, "Organizational Learning Processes and Outcomes: Major Findings and Future Research Directions," Management Science, vol. 67, no. 9, pp. 5399–5429, 2021.
7. J. A. Wagner III and J. R. Hollenbeck, Organizational Behavior: Securing Competitive Advantage. Routledge, 2020.
8. M. A. Camilleri, "Using the Balanced Scorecard as a Performance Management Tool in Higher Education," Management in Education, vol. 35, no. 1, pp. 10–21, 2021.

CHAPTER 6

The Contraction of Primary and Secondary Industries vs. the Expansion of the Tertiary Industry

6.1 The Contraction of Primary and Secondary Industries

Karl Marx's assertion that "machines eat men" reveals that while technological advancements have increased productivity, they have also inevitably squeezed the living space of laborers. As technology evolves, especially in productive industries, the introduction of automation and artificial intelligence (AI) has continuously improved production efficiency, while human workers have gradually lost their jobs in the process. The rise of autonomous driving technology is a typical example. Autonomous vehicles, with their advantages of tirelessness, low costs, energy efficiency, and superior safety, are rapidly taking over the market, replacing numerous jobs traditionally held by human drivers. It is foreseeable that taxi drivers will struggle to resist this technological tide, and they may eventually face widespread unemployment, further validating Marx's "machines eat men" assertion (Fig. 6.1).

The demand for robots and automation technology is not only increasing in the taxi industry but across all production-oriented sectors. This growing demand reduces the need for human labor, leading to a dramatic contraction in the job market. This shift in the employment landscape brings severe social issues: large numbers of workers may find themselves unable to secure jobs, leading to increased social inequality, a widening wealth gap, and a series of social conflicts. This situation forces

X. Cao, *Modern Business Management*,
https://doi.org/10.1007/978-981-96-0594-1_6

Fig. 6.1 Machines replace human jobs as technological progress leads to higher efficiency

us to reflect on our future in this rapidly changing technological era: Are we creating a world that is pushing us toward the brink of unemployment?

However, the issue is not that simple. In the long run, robots, AI, and automation are indeed gradually replacing human roles in production processes, especially in jobs that can be precisely quantified and have clear, objective standards. For instance, robots can perform tasks more efficiently and accurately in manufacturing assembly lines and driving in transportation. As a result, human labor in these industries will gradually be phased out.

6.2 The Expansion of the Tertiary Industry

As you pointed out, there are still areas where robots cannot easily replace humans, particularly those with a high degree of subjectivity and human touch. Fields like psychological counseling, handicrafts, and artistic creation are characterized by their difficulty in being precisely quantified or defined by objective standards. Psychological counseling requires a deep understanding of human emotions and mental states, something that cannot be fully achieved through data analysis and logical reasoning alone. Handcrafted art often reflects the personal emotions and unique aesthetic of the creator, making the creation process itself an irreplaceable form of artistic expression. In the restaurant industry, the emphasis on "handmade" not only refers to the process but also to the cultural and emotional transmission behind it.

Therefore, humans have natural advantages in these fields, primarily because "people are people," endowed with emotions, creativity, and subjectivity. These traits ensure that certain aspects of human work can never be fully replaced by machines. Although automation and AI will surpass humans in more and more areas in the long term, fields requiring emotional resonance, personalized service, and artistic expression will still rely heavily on human involvement. For example, in a restaurant emphasizing handmade and personalized service or cultural and emotional transmission, even the most advanced robots would struggle to compete.

While the development of automation and AI is undoubtedly challenging humanity's role in traditional production industries, humans still hold an irreplaceable advantage in sectors that are difficult to quantify and have a high degree of subjectivity and human touch. This suggests that in the future occupational structure, we may see more growth in the tertiary sector, particularly in industries emphasizing personalized and human-centric services, which will become crucial employment areas for human workers.

6.3 Career Choices for the Future

In light of the trends described above, career choices, educational directions, and mindset adjustments for the future need to be reconsidered and planned within the context of rapid technological advancement.

Firstly, in terms of career choice, we should focus more on areas that are not easily replaceable by machines and AI. As automation becomes more prevalent in production industries, traditional manual labor and repetitive tasks will increasingly be taken over by robots. Therefore, people should lean toward careers requiring creativity, emotional investment, and interpersonal interaction. Professions such as psychological counselors, artists, teachers, and craftsmen not only demand professional skills but also require a deep understanding of human emotions and personalized needs. Due to the high degree of subjectivity and human touch in these fields, machines struggle to perform these roles, making them more competitive in the future job market. Additionally, as society's demand for high-quality services and personalized experiences grows, high-end service industries like fine dining, custom services, and health management will see broad development opportunities, making them worth considering as career paths (Fig. 6.2).

Secondly, in terms of educational choices, future students should focus more on interdisciplinary learning and the development of comprehensive abilities. Traditional disciplinary boundaries are becoming increasingly blurred, and future job demands will lean more toward integrated, cross-field talent. Therefore, in addition to choosing technical majors with broad application prospects, students should also consider studying humanities, art design, sociology, and other fields, especially emerging disciplines that combine these areas with technology, such as digital humanities and intelligent design. These majors not only cultivate professional skills but also enhance creativity, critical thinking, and communication skills, making graduates more adaptable in their future careers.

Faced with the constantly changing social and occupational environment, we also need to adjust our mindsets to adapt to future uncertainties. The acceleration of technological change and shifts in the job market require us to possess flexible adaptability, with lifelong learning being the core. Future workers cannot rely solely on one-time educational knowledge but must continually learn and update their skills to meet evolving job demands. Whether through formal education systems, online courses, or professional training, we must stay sensitive to new knowledge and technology, proactively learning and mastering new skills. This attitude of lifelong learning will be key to future career success.

Moreover, we must recognize that as members of society, we should not only witness the development of future technologies but actively participate in them. Technological progress must align with human values to ensure social harmony and progress. In the future, finding ways to

Fig. 6.2 Changing career preferences among future graduates: fields related to the primary and secondary industries are gradually losing appeal, while those related to the tertiary sector are becoming more popular

mitigate the impact of automation on employment through policy, social mechanisms, and public engagement, while ensuring human-centered technological applications, will be a collective challenge. We should all actively engage in this dialogue between technology and humanity to guide technology in a direction that benefits society as a whole.

In conclusion, facing the challenges posed by automation and AI, we need to focus on creativity and human-centric fields in career choices, emphasize interdisciplinary learning and comprehensive ability development in education, and maintain adaptability and lifelong learning awareness in our mindset. At the same time, we must actively participate in the social dialogue between technology and humanity, ensuring that technological progress remains centered on human needs. These thoughts and actions will help us find our place in the future, avoid the risk of unemployment, and maximize personal value.

We need to shift our thinking to actively adapt to this service-centered economic model. First, improving service awareness and skills is crucial. Future society will place greater emphasis on interpersonal interaction and personalized experiences, requiring professionals in retail, dining, education, healthcare, and other fields to have excellent communication skills and service abilities. This not only determines customer satisfaction but directly impacts personal career development. Second, building interpersonal networks is essential. Future society will heavily depend on interpersonal interaction, and good relationships can lead to more career opportunities and business expansion possibilities. By participating in industry events and utilizing social media to expand connections, we can better integrate into this field. Meanwhile, cultural literacy improvement is also indispensable. As the cultural industry grows in the tertiary sector, professionals need a deep understanding of culture, history, and art to make their services more profound and appealing. Additionally, mastering digital tools and technology can significantly enhance work efficiency and service quality, helping us stand out in the competition. On this basis, we should also focus on sustainability and social responsibility, ensuring that we create greater value for society while providing quality services. Continuous learning and professional development are long-term ways to stay competitive in the rapidly changing tertiary sector. Through these efforts, we can find our place in the tertiary sector and maximize our personal value.

References

1. A. Henry, Understanding Strategic Management. Oxford University Press, 2021.
2. S. Gupta, V. A. Drave, Y. K. Dwivedi, et al., "Achieving Superior Organizational Performance via Big Data Predictive Analytics: A Dynamic Capability View," Industrial Marketing Management, vol. 90, pp. 581–592, 2020.
3. O. Shenkar, Y. Luo, and T. Chi, International Business. Routledge, 2021.
4. K. Black, Business Statistics: For Contemporary Decision Making. John Wiley & Sons, 2023.

5. S. Aujirpongpan and Y. Hareebin, "The Effect of Strategic Intuition, Business Analytics, Networking Capabilities, and Dynamic Strategy on Innovation Performance: The Empirical Study Thai Processed Food Exporters," The Journal of Asian Finance, Economics and Business, vol. 7, no. 1, pp. 259–268, 2020.
6. R. Staring and R. van Swaaningen, Borders, Mobilities, and Governance in Transnational Perspective. Oxford Research Encyclopedia of Criminology and Criminal Justice, 2021.
7. T. R. Hughes and F. D. Davidson, "Deconstructing Strategic Planning: Time to Retain, Revise, or Retire?," The Palgrave Handbook of Educational Leadership and Management Discourse: 1–21, 2020.
8. L. Argote, S. Lee, and J. Park, "Organizational Learning Processes and Outcomes: Major Findings and Future Research Directions," Management Science, vol. 67, no. 9, pp. 5399–5429, 2021.

CHAPTER 7

Moore's Law and Endless Desires

7.1 Moore's Law: Growth on the Supply Side

Moore's Law states that the density of integrated circuits doubles every 24 months, while the cost is halved. Since its introduction in 1965, this principle has accurately described the development trajectory of computer technology. Moore's Law has driven rapid growth in computing speed, storage capacity, and graphics processing capabilities, leading to significant technological advancements. People once expected these improvements to greatly enhance our work efficiency and everyday lives, making operations smoother. However, the notable increase in hardware performance has not fully translated into a revolutionary change in user experience. The reason behind this lies not only in the pace of technological progress but also in the rapid expansion of human demands and desires, making it difficult for hardware advancements to fully meet users' expectations (Fig. 7.1).

Since the mid-twentieth century, Moore's Law has been a driving force behind technological progress. Over the past few decades, the speed of computer processors has increased from a few hundred megahertz to several thousand megahertz, and the capacities of memory and hard drives have also experienced similar exponential growth. These technological breakthroughs have made previously unimaginable tasks, such as real-time video rendering, complex scientific calculations, and massive data

X. Cao, *Modern Business Management*,
https://doi.org/10.1007/978-981-96-0594-1_7

Fig. 7.1 Moore's Law illustrates how hardware performance, including integrated circuits, has exponentially increased over time

processing, entirely feasible. At the same time, the advances in information technology driven by Moore's Law have facilitated the widespread adoption of the internet and the rapid rise of mobile computing. As the computing power and speed of computers continue to improve, it has fueled our optimism for future technology.

Despite the significant increase in hardware performance, looking back, we find that user experience has not improved as dramatically as expected. While the computational power and speed of computers have consistently increased, the improvement in user experience has not been proportional.

For instance, the enhancements in webpage loading speeds and gaming fluidity have not kept pace with the growth in hardware performance, reflecting a gap between technological progress and user expectations.

7.2 The Unbounded Desires: Growth on the Demand Side

One key reason for this is that human desires and needs are growing at a rate that surpasses the increase in hardware performance. Although Moore's Law ensures that hardware performance doubles every few years, people's demands for faster speeds, higher resolutions, and more complex functionalities are multiplying in even shorter periods. For example, while we were once satisfied with low-resolution video playback, today, 4K or even 8K ultra-high-definition streaming has become the standard. Similarly, we are no longer content with basic webpage loading speeds; instead, we expect dynamic content to load instantly and respond in milliseconds (Fig. 7.2).

This expansion of desires comes at a high cost. Although Moore's Law continues to drive hardware performance improvements, the increasing complexity of software has significantly diminished the benefits of these hardware enhancements. As hardware capabilities grow, software developers design more powerful and visually sophisticated applications. These programs are often large in size and demand substantial computing resources. Modern operating systems can easily take up tens of gigabytes, and commonly used software may require several gigabytes of memory to run smoothly. As a result, the improvements in hardware performance may not always translate into a noticeable enhancement in user experience. In some cases, the load times may even increase. For instance, browsers today are equipped with features such as ad blocking, privacy protection, and video playback. Although these features enhance the functionality of the browser, they also significantly increase its demand for computing resources.

7.3 The Escalation of Imbalance

The improvement in hardware performance and the growth in human desires have created a "dynamic competition." Every leap in hardware performance generates new demands, which, in turn, drive the development of even higher-performing hardware. However, the rate at which

Fig. 7.2 The unbounded expansion of human desires, such as our pursuit of more health, rights, love, freedom, and happiness

desires grow often outpaces the improvement in hardware performance. When hardware is upgraded, people quickly shift their focus to more complex applications, higher visual standards, or greater interactivity, thus consuming the potential benefits of the hardware upgrades. This reveals a fundamental truth: although hardware performance has made significant strides, achieving a revolutionary leap in user experience remains elusive.

Moore's Law has accelerated the rapid development of the information society, but it still cannot keep pace with the continuous escalation of human desires. The increasing complexity of software and the growing demands for speed and functionality mean that hardware improvements do not always result in better user experiences. While technological progress is important, we must also manage and optimize software design and maintain realistic expectations about the benefits technology can deliver. Otherwise, the performance gains promised by Moore's Law will always be chasing after the expanding scope of human desires.

Moreover, from an entrepreneurial perspective, the growth in product demand is ongoing and will not be fully satisfied by short-term technological advancements. For instance, some early commentators believed that once computer performance reached a certain level, the demand for home computers would stabilize, and there would be no need for further significant improvements. However, in reality, as technology progresses, people's demands for extreme performance in computing devices have not subsided but rather continued to grow. Technological advancements have not curbed demand; instead, they have fueled the human desire for ever-greater performance.

7.4 The Paradox of Desire and Technological Progress

Looking back at the development of human society, we observe that desires have continuously evolved alongside improvements in material conditions. From basic survival needs to the pursuit of a refined lifestyle, human desires seem to never be fully satisfied. This phenomenon is not only apparent in daily life but also in technological advancements. For example, in China fifty years ago, people primarily sought to meet their basic needs for food and clothing. Today, with the improvement of social productivity, people's demands have shifted from mere survival to a higher quality of life, such as better food and more sophisticated consumer experiences. This upgrading of demands reflects humanity's constant pursuit of higher levels of satisfaction, a trend that appears to be endless.

As productivity improves, the supply of goods and services continues to increase, but human desires always outpace supply. Every technological advancement sparks new demands, and these demands often exceed the rate of productivity growth. Moore's Law in the computing field is a prime example of this. Despite the significant improvement in hardware performance, human demands have grown exponentially, if not faster. As computers evolve from word processing to multimedia handling and now to artificial intelligence, each hardware upgrade is met with even higher expectations. It becomes increasingly difficult for technological advancements to keep up with the ever-expanding desires.

7.5 The Desire-Driven Cycle

The growth of human desires not only manifests in daily life but also profoundly influences consumption behavior. Take computers and smartphones as examples. Despite continuous improvements in device performance, which theoretically should satisfy users' needs and reduce the frequency of replacements, in reality, new technological standards, faster processing speeds, and updated features constantly fuel consumer desire for new products. This continuous upgrading of desires drives the consumption cycle: performance improvements satisfy current needs but simultaneously generate new desires, further pushing technological development.

The relationship between technological progress and human desire resembles a dual driving force: every technological breakthrough generates new demands, which, in turn, prompt the development of more advanced technologies. But what is the ultimate desire of humanity? From the current perspective, it seems that desires have no limit. We always strive for faster speeds, stronger performance, and even exploration of unknown territories, such as life extension or consciousness uploading. This relentless pursuit of the unknown and higher realms not only drives technological progress but also brings new challenges to society.

The technological leaps driven by Moore's Law reveal an undeniable reality: human desires are always ahead of technology. Even as technology advances, we continue to create new demands, making it impossible for technological progress to fully satisfy them. This insatiable desire is the very force propelling society and technology forward. Therefore, the enhancement of computer and smartphone performance will not halt our pursuit; rather, it will fuel our desire for even greater performance. It is this endless desire that drives the continuous advancement of both technology and society.

References

1. G. E. Moore, "Cramming More Components onto Integrated Circuits," Electronics, vol. 38, no. 8, pp. 114–117, 1965.
2. M. M. Waldrop, "The Chips Are Down for Moore's Law," Nature, vol. 530,

no. 7589, pp. 144–147, 2016.
3. G. Marsh, "Moore's Law at the Extremes," Materials Today, vol. 6, no. 5, pp. 28–33, 2003.
4. S. Borkar and A. A. Chien, "The Future of Microprocessors," Communications of the ACM, vol. 54, no. 5, pp. 67–77, 2011.
5. R. R. Schaller, "Moore's Law: Past, Present and Future," IEEE Spectrum, vol. 34, no. 6, pp. 52–59, 1997.
6. J. Shalf, "The Future of Computing Beyond Moore's Law," Philosophical Transactions of the Royal Society A, vol. 378, no. 2166, Art no. 20190061, 2020.
7. A. Tibazarwa, "Strategic Integration for Hardware and Software Convergence Complexity," IEEE Engineering Management Review, vol. 49, no. 3, pp. 92–102, 2021.
8. L. Bertalanffy, General System Theory: Foundations, Development, Applications, 1969.
9. R. J. Mitchell, Ed., Managing Complexity in Software Engineering, no. 17. IET, 1990.
10. T. Ciarli, M. Kenney, S. Massini, et al., "Digital Technologies, Innovation, and Skills: Emerging Trajectories and Challenges," Research Policy, vol. 50, no. 7, Art no. 104289, 2021.

CHAPTER 8

The Moore's Law in the Field of Artificial Intelligence

8.1 ChatGPT: The Dark Horse of 2023 and the Dawn of a New Era in AI

In 2023, the field of artificial intelligence (AI) witnessed a monumental breakthrough with the emergence of ChatGPT. Developed by OpenAI, this Artificial General Intelligence (AGI) model, with its powerful natural language processing capabilities and lifelike conversational experience, shocked the world. ChatGPT is more than just a tool; it symbolizes an era, representing significant progress in the field of AGI. With the success of ChatGPT, humanity has, for the first time, tangibly felt the profound impact of AI, prompting deep societal reflections on the future (Fig. 8.1).

A new AI Moore's Law is quietly making its way into our daily lives. Sam Altman, CEO of OpenAI, proposed a new "Moore's Law"—the level of AI intelligence doubles every 18 months. This statement has sparked widespread discussion and attention. Altman's viewpoint is based on the rapid iteration and progress of AI technology, particularly in the training and application of large models, where AI's performance and capabilities have seen significant enhancements in a short period. This exponential growth suggests that AI's development trajectory will far surpass the progress of traditional computer hardware, becoming a new driving force for future technological advancements. This new "Moore's Law" reveals a striking reality: AI capabilities are advancing rapidly, achieving in months what once took years or even decades. This speed not only accelerates

X. Cao, *Modern Business Management*,
https://doi.org/10.1007/978-981-96-0594-1_8

Fig. 8.1 General AI technology, represented by ChatGPT, is drastically impacting and reshaping our lives

the proliferation of AI technology but also deepens concerns about AI's potential impacts (Fig. 8.2).

When discussing AI intelligence, the Turing Test is an unavoidable concept. Proposed by computer scientist Alan Turing in 1950, this test is used to determine whether a machine possesses human-like intelligence. The core idea of the Turing Test is that if a machine can engage in conversation indistinguishably from a human, it can be considered to have human-level intelligence. In the past, the Turing Test was seen as the ultimate challenge in AI, with only a few specific tasks and scenarios

Fig. 8.2 Large language models, represented by ChatGPT, have successfully passed the Turing Test in various scenarios, heralding a new era

where AI could barely pass. Today, however, large language models like ChatGPT have successfully passed the Turing Test in various scenarios. These models not only understand and generate natural language but also exhibit human-like thinking patterns and emotional responses in conversations. This breakthrough marks a significant milestone, ushering AI into a new era of human-level intelligence. Although the Turing Test is not without its flaws, it remains an important benchmark for assessing AI intelligence. The success of large models like ChatGPT in passing the Turing Test indicates that AI's abilities in understanding, generating, and interacting have reached new heights. These models can not only perform complex language tasks but also display creativity and logical reasoning in certain situations, leading humanity to reconsider the future direction of AI development.

8.2 The Growing Gap Between Human and AI Intelligence

As AI capabilities continue to advance, the intelligence gap between humans and AI is rapidly widening. While AI intelligence is making leaps and bounds, human cognitive abilities—such as brainpower, IQ, memory, and information processing—show little sign of significant improvement in the short term. This stark contrast highlights the rapid rise of AI, while human intelligence may have reached a bottleneck (Fig. 8.3).

First, AI's computational power is growing exponentially. Take ChatGPT as an example: the computational resources and algorithms behind it are constantly being optimized, with the computational power used during training reaching unprecedented levels. In comparison, while the human brain is complex, it has not seen significant improvement in computational capacity in recent decades. AI algorithms can process vast amounts of data in a short time and extract useful information, whereas humans often rely on intuition and experience when faced with complex data, making AI more efficient and accurate in many tasks.

Second, AI's learning speed far surpasses that of humans. During training, large models can rapidly absorb vast amounts of data and enhance their capabilities through continuous iteration and optimization. In contrast, human learning is relatively slow, constrained by innate conditions, environmental factors, and educational levels. AI can achieve in weeks or months what takes humans decades to learn, making AI superior to human experts in many fields.

Finally, AI's memory and information storage capacity far exceed that of humans. Although the human brain boasts a complex neural network and highly flexible thinking, it cannot compete with AI in terms of memory capacity and information processing speed. AI can store and retrieve vast amounts of data with almost no concept of forgetting, while human memory is limited and easily influenced by emotions, stress, and other factors. This gives AI an unparalleled advantage in handling large-scale information.

Fig. 8.3 As AI intelligence increases, human intelligence faces potential threats, with many worrying about whether AI will eventually subjugate humanity

8.3 Reflections on the Future: Optimism or Worry?

Faced with this reality, it is difficult to maintain an optimistic outlook on the future of humanity. The rapid pace of AI development and its profound impact exceed the expectations of many. While AI brings numerous opportunities and conveniences, its potential threats cannot be ignored. How to maintain the core values and status of humanity in an era of rapid AI development is a significant challenge we must face.

First, the rapid development of AI may bring ethical and moral challenges. As AI increasingly participates in various aspects of human society, from healthcare and finance to education and law, ensuring that AI's decisions are just and ethical becomes a pressing issue. AI decisions rely on vast data sets, but the sources, processing methods, and outcomes may differ from human moral standards, potentially leading to social injustice.

Second, the impact of AI on the job market is also a cause for concern. As AI continues to advance in automation and intelligence, many traditional jobs may be replaced. Although AI will also create new job opportunities, it will be a significant challenge for workers whose skills do not match these new demands to find their place in the rapidly changing job market. Society needs to prepare for this, offering necessary training and re-education to help workers adapt to the new economic environment.

Additionally, the safety and controllability of AI cannot be overlooked. As AI capabilities increase, so does the scope and complexity of its autonomous decision-making. Ensuring that AI does not deviate from human intentions during task execution and preventing AI from being used for malicious purposes have become global focal points. The transparency, explainability, and controllability of AI need greater emphasis to ensure that its use does not negatively impact society.

Lastly, the rise of AI brings philosophical considerations about human identity and meaning. As AI surpasses humans in certain areas, many are beginning to question humanity's place and significance in future society. Will we be replaced by AI? Do human creativity, emotions, and moral values still hold irreplaceable significance? These questions are not merely technical but involve how humanity redefines its existence and value in the context of rapidly advancing technology.

The success of ChatGPT in 2023 marks a new stage for AI. While this progress showcases the enormous potential of technology, it also brings numerous challenges and uncertainties. As we enjoy the conveniences brought by AI, we must also calmly think about and address potential risks, ensuring that humanity can still control its destiny in the future world.

8.4 Re-examining Human Existence

Throughout the long history of human development, we have experienced several significant psychological setbacks that gradually dismantled our perception of humanity's unique place in the universe. Each setback forced us to reevaluate ourselves and redefine our existence. Today, with the advent of general large models represented by ChatGPT and the exponential growth of AI intelligence, humanity is about to face its fourth major psychological setback. This setback challenges our understanding of intelligence and suggests that we may further diminish our perception of ourselves.

8.4.1 *The First Setback: Copernicus's Heliocentric Theory*

The first major setback came from Copernicus's heliocentric theory. Before Copernicus, humanity firmly believed that the Earth was the center of the universe, with the Sun, Moon, and all the stars revolving around it. This geocentric view was not only a scientific belief but also a reflection of humanity's self-centered consciousness. We believed the Earth was our home, and we were the masters of all things, with the rest of the universe merely serving as a backdrop. However, Copernicus's heliocentric theory completely overturned this belief. He proposed that the Earth was not the center of the universe; rather, the Sun was the center of the solar system, and the Earth was merely a planet orbiting it. This theory shook humanity's belief in its unique place in the universe, forcing us to acknowledge that Earth is but a speck of dust in the vast cosmos, making human existence seem insignificant.

8.4.2 *The Second Setback: Darwin's Theory of Evolution*

The second major psychological setback came from Darwin's theory of evolution. Before Darwin, humanity generally believed that it was a creation of God, fundamentally different from other animals and the "crown of creation." We believed that our intelligence, morality, and spirituality far surpassed other beings, justifying our place at the top of the Earth's food chain. Darwin's theory of evolution shattered this illusion. Through extensive research and evidence, Darwin pointed out that humans are not fundamentally different from other animals; we are merely a link in the evolutionary chain, gradually evolving through natural selection. This realization degraded humanity from a divine creation to a species sharing a common ancestor with apes. This shift in understanding dealt another blow to our perception of our uniqueness (Fig. 8.4).

Fig. 8.4 Copernicus's heliocentric theory, Darwin's theory of evolution, Freud's psychoanalysis, and the rise of AI surpassing human intelligence have all dealt significant blows to humanity, severely undermining our confidence

8.4.3 *The Third Setback: Freud's Psychoanalysis*

The third major setback came from Freud's psychoanalytic theory, particularly his views in The Interpretation of Dreams. For a long time, humanity believed that its fundamental distinction from other animals and machines lay in our independent consciousness, complex emotions, and rich subjective experiences. We believed that our thoughts and emotions were unique, marking us as a higher form of life. Freud's research showed that the human mind is far from the independent and autonomous entity we imagined. Dreams, the subconscious, and various mental activities can be objectively analyzed and are even subject to biological and psychological influences. The emotions and consciousness we pride ourselves on are merely products of psychological mechanisms, often influenced and controlled by external factors without our awareness. This discovery forced humanity to acknowledge that our mental world is not as mysterious and unique as we thought and can even be considered partially "mechanical."

8.4.4 *The Fourth Setback: The Rise of Artificial Intelligence*

Today, with the widespread application of general large models like ChatGPT, humanity is on the verge of facing its fourth major psychological setback. We once believed that intelligence was a uniquely human trait, the key factor that made us the rulers of the Earth. Whether it was our complex language abilities, creativity, or reasoning skills, we used these to distinguish humans from other species. However, the advent of ChatGPT and other AI models challenges this deeply ingrained belief. ChatGPT can not only engage in fluent natural language conversation but also perform complex reasoning, creation, and decision-making, even surpassing human abilities in some aspects. More importantly, AI's intelligence level is increasing exponentially, doubling every 18 months, far outpacing the evolution and learning speed of the human brain. All of this suggests that the uniqueness of human intelligence is facing an unprecedented challenge. The intelligence advantage we once prided ourselves on may soon be overtaken by AI. As AI becomes widely used across various fields, humanity will have to accept the reality that we are no longer the sole possessors of intelligence, nor the smartest species on Earth.

From Copernicus's heliocentric theory to Darwin's theory of evolution, and from Freud's psychoanalysis to the rise of AI, humanity has experienced a series of cognitive setbacks throughout history, each time forcing us to downgrade our perception of ourselves. Now, with the rise of AI, we are about to face the fourth major psychological setback. This time, AI not only challenges our definition of intelligence but also forces us to reconsider our place in the world and the universe.

Faced with this pessimistic reality, what we need is not just control over technology but a deep reflection on ourselves. How can humanity maintain its uniqueness in the age of AI? How can we redefine the concept of "intelligence"? How can we find a new place in this rapidly changing world? These are questions we must seriously consider.

Like every previous setback in history, this challenge may also become an opportunity for human progress. By confronting the challenges brought by AI and exploring the true meaning of human intelligence, we may find a way to preserve our value in a world of rapidly advancing technology. However, this process will be fraught with pain and confusion, forcing us to redefine our existence in a constantly changing world.

8.5 Reconsidering Humanity

In today's technological age, with the rapid development of AI and the widespread application of robotics, humanity faces unprecedented challenges. We are gradually realizing that our advantages in physical and intellectual abilities are being surpassed by machines. This situation compels us to ask: If we no longer hold the advantage in these areas, what unique advantages do we have left? Will our jobs be replaced by AI? On a deeper level, what does the future hold for us? These questions are not only about technology but also concern social structure, wealth distribution, and the value of humanity itself.

First, we must acknowledge that our traditional advantages in physical and intellectual capacities are facing severe challenges. Modern robots far surpass humans in physical strength and can perform various high-intensity and repetitive tasks. At the same time, AI exhibits extraordinary capabilities in processing information, performing complex calculations, and making decisions. Whether in data analysis or language understanding, AI can accomplish tasks faster and more accurately than humans. In this context, our traditional advantages are gradually weakening, forcing us to reassess our roles.

Looking back at history, we once believed that wars and social conflicts were caused by resource shortages. However, modern wars have not decreased with the improvement of productivity; instead, they are often exacerbated by unequal resource distribution. Similarly, unemployment is not merely due to insufficient productivity. In reality, unemployment in modern society is often related to overproduction. When productivity increases significantly and the number of products grows, society does not necessarily become more prosperous. This is because the wealth and resources produced are not distributed equitably, leaving some people unable to enjoy the benefits of technological progress.

Faced with this reality, the core issue lies not in technological progress itself but in the distribution of wealth. The widespread application of robots and AI is not the root cause of unemployment. The real challenge is how to fairly distribute the wealth and outcomes brought by technology. In a society with highly developed productivity, ensuring that everyone can fairly share in the benefits of technological progress is the key issue we need to address.

Imagine a future "Great Unity Society" where robots and AI serve humanity, significantly improving productivity and quality of life. If these technological advances can lead to equitable distribution of social wealth, allowing everyone to enjoy the fruits of what robots create, it would be an ideal state. In such a scenario, humans could be freed from arduous work and focus on creative, social, and spiritual development.

To achieve this ideal, we need to establish and improve a fair wealth distribution system. Governments and societies must actively explore new distribution methods to ensure that the wealth created by technological progress truly benefits everyone. This may include raising social security levels, implementing universal basic income, and improving education and training systems to help people adapt to the job requirements of the new economy.

In conclusion, while the rapid development of AI and robotics indeed significantly impacts the traditional job market and social structure, these challenges also provide us with an opportunity to reevaluate and improve our social systems. We must recognize that issues like unemployment and wealth inequality are not direct results of technological progress but rather flaws in the existing wealth distribution system. The key to the future lies in balancing technological progress with social welfare, ensuring that everyone can benefit from the advancements in technology. Only in this way can we find a new path in a challenging era and realize a more equitable and better society.

References

1. A. M. Turing, Computing Machinery and Intelligence. Springer Netherlands, 2009.
2. J. Shalf, "The future of Computing Beyond Moore's Law," Philosophical Transactions of the Royal Society A, vol. 378, no. 2166, p. 20190061, 2020.
3. G. E. Moore, "Cramming More Components onto Integrated Circuits," Proceedings of the IEEE, vol. 86, no. 1, pp. 82–85, 1998.
4. M. M. Waldrop, "The Chips Are Down for Moore's Law," Nature News, vol. 530, no. 7589, p. 144, 2016.
5. R. R. Schaller, "Moore's Law: Past, Present and Future," IEEE Spectrum, vol. 34, no. 6, pp. 52–59, 1997.
6. S. Borkar and A. A. Chien, "The Future of Microprocessors," Communications of the ACM, vol. 54, no. 5, pp. 67–77, 2011.
7. G. Marsh, "Moore's Law at the Extremes," Materials Today, vol. 6, no. 5, pp. 28–33, 2003.
8. T. Ciarli, M. Kenney, S. Massini, et al., "Digital Technologies, Innovation, and Skills: Emerging Trajectories and Challenges," Research Policy, vol. 50, no. 7, p. 104289, 2021.
9. J. H. Holland, Adaptation in Natural and Artificial Systems: An Introductory Analysis with Applications to Biology, Control, and Artificial Intelligence. MIT Press, 1992.
10. K. J. Cios, W. Pedrycz, R. W. Swiniarski, et al., Data Mining and Knowledge Discovery. Springer US, 1998.
11. N. J. Nilsson, Artificial Intelligence: A New Synthesis. Morgan Kaufmann, 1998.
12. M. Mitchell, Complexity: A Guided Tour. Oxford University Press, 2009.
13. R. S. Sutton, Reinforcement Learning: An Introduction. A Bradford Book, 2018.

CHAPTER 9

Lessons from the Extinction of Dinosaurs

9.1 A Historical Review of Dinosaur Extinction

The extinction of dinosaurs is one of the most significant mass extinction events in Earth's history, occurring around 66 million years ago at the end of the Cretaceous period. Scientists widely believe that this event was primarily caused by a massive asteroid impact on Earth. This impact brought about dramatic climate changes, severely affecting Earth's ecosystems (Fig. 9.1).

Before the extinction of dinosaurs, Earth's ecosystem was in a state of "incremental growth." During this period, abundant plant life, including ferns and early angiosperms, converted solar energy into biomass through photosynthesis, forming a rich food chain. This plentiful plant resource supported a large number of herbivorous dinosaurs, which in turn provided ample prey for carnivorous dinosaurs. The large size of these dinosaurs gave them a significant advantage in the ecosystem at that time (Fig. 9.2).

However, approximately 66 million years ago, Earth was struck by an asteroid, an event that had profound effects on the planet's environment. The impact triggered global wildfires and released vast amounts of dust and gases into the atmosphere, blocking sunlight. This blockage led to a sudden drop in global temperatures, disrupting photosynthesis, which in turn hindered plant growth and collapsed the entire food chain.

X. Cao, *Modern Business Management*,
https://doi.org/10.1007/978-981-96-0594-1_9

Fig. 9.1 Before the asteroid impact, dinosaurs were at the top of the food chain, dominating the ecosystem. Their large size and strength were fully displayed in that era, similar to how companies pursue expansion, listing, and capital accumulation during periods of economic growth

9.2 Economic Transformation: Lessons from Dinosaur Extinction

Before the asteroid impact, Earth's ecosystem was thriving in a "world of incremental growth," where the abundance of plants and biomass provided ample food resources for large animals. Dinosaurs, as the largest terrestrial animals of that time, had the advantage of size, which allowed

Fig. 9.2 After the asteroid impact, dinosaurs struggled in the harsh environment, weakened by food shortages and starvation. This scenario mirrors the bleak atmosphere of an economic downturn, highlighting the dinosaurs' powerlessness in the face of extreme survival challenges

them to dominate in a food-rich environment. However, the climate upheaval caused by the impact transformed Earth's environment into a "world of shrinking resources," where the supply of energy and resources significantly dwindled. In this new environment, the reduction of plant life led to the collapse of the food chain. Large dinosaurs, with their massive bodies and enormous energy needs, could no longer find enough food and resources to survive. In contrast, smaller organisms, such as early mammals, could survive on less food and energy, giving them an advantage in this new environment.

This concept can be applied to modern economics, particularly in the context of China's significant economic downturn. The incremental growth stage in economics refers to a period of vigorous economic activity, where markets and businesses enjoy abundant growth opportunities and resources. In such a scenario, large corporations or investment institutions, like dinosaurs, can leverage their size and resource advantages to capture more market share and economic benefits.

However, when the economic environment shifts to a "world of shrinking resources," such as during economic downturns, reduced market demand, or policy adjustments, resources and opportunities become scarce. At this time, the advantages of large companies may turn into liabilities because they require higher fixed costs and larger resource inputs. Conversely, smaller companies or agile investment institutions can adapt more quickly to changes, reduce costs, and may even find greater opportunities for survival in this environment.

The extinction of dinosaurs shows that environmental changes have profound impacts on the survival of species. Similarly, changes in the economic environment can affect the survival and development of businesses. In the face of economic downturns or policy transitions, large companies may need to adjust their strategies to adapt to the new environment, while agile small businesses may find new opportunities in the changed economic conditions.

Before the asteroid impact, Earth's ecosystem was similar to the pre-2024 economic environment in China. Since 2000, China's economy has experienced rapid growth, with the national GDP growing at an annual rate of 8%. China gradually became a global manufacturing hub, playing a crucial role in the global supply chain. Startups emerged rapidly, and entrepreneurship became a common topic of conversation among university students. For young people, especially those in the IT industry, turning their technical skills into startup projects was highly appealing. For those already engaged in entrepreneurship, interacting with various investment institutions and participating in roadshows organized by local governments and investment bodies became a new norm. Funding rounds like angel, Series A, and Series B were never short of money, only lacking good projects, and even good ideas could attract financing. In a high-growth economic environment where entrepreneurship, fundraising, and listing were the goals of many ambitious youths, everyone was chasing expansion and leveraging capital, much like the pursuit of "faster, higher, stronger" in the Olympics. At that time, no one questioned the goal of building a big and strong company, and few considered focusing on being small but specialized. In contrast, overseas markets were relatively calm. For example, in the field of computing, many open-source projects, particularly in artificial intelligence, could easily be found on platforms like GitHub. Many smart domestic entrepreneurs quickly adapted these overseas open-source projects for financing, successfully securing initial investments in China. Similar projects, if not in China, would either remain quietly on GitHub or be placed on crowdfunding sites like Kickstarter to receive limited overseas investments.

However, by 2024, the deterioration of Sino-US relations and the global overcapacity environment triggered a series of chain reactions. Falling housing prices, rising unemployment rates, increasing deflation, and more conservative institutional investments, especially those with state-owned capital backgrounds, became more cautious. Even though the central bank lowered reserve requirements and interest rates and accelerated printing money, the banking system's loans could not be absorbed by the market, remaining idle in institutions. The pursuit of success cooled down, and the "lie flat" mentality gained traction. In the context of economic bubbles bursting, policy adjustments, or declining market demand, companies need to quickly adapt to new policies and market environments. Comprehensive policy transitions, such as increased corporate buyback responsibilities and strengthened financial regulations, can pose new challenges and pressures for businesses. Companies need to reevaluate their business models, cost structures, and market strategies to adapt to new economic conditions. Economic slowdowns lead to decreased consumer confidence and reduced demand, resulting in declining sales, inventory buildup, and intensified market competition. Companies may face reduced revenue and increased sales pressure. Due to reduced sales and rising costs, profit margins are compressed, putting financial pressure on many companies, even leading to losses. Increased uncertainty leads businesses and investors to reduce capital expenditures and investments, affecting long-term economic growth potential. Reduced corporate investment may hinder future development opportunities and innovation capabilities. Corporate layoffs and downsizing lead to higher unemployment rates, affecting social stability. The unemployment problem exacerbates consumer shrinkage, further impacting economic growth. Companies face increased debt repayment pressure, and banks may encounter rising non-performing loans, posing potential financial instability risks.

Against the backdrop of China's economic downturn, the impact on people's livelihoods is significant, manifesting in various aspects. Economic slowdown leads to reduced corporate hiring, especially for young people and new graduates, who face greater employment pressure. Tight job markets directly affect household income and social stability. Slow or stagnant income growth makes it difficult for households to improve their living standards, affecting consumer spending and quality of life, further exacerbating economic downturn pressures. Economic uncertainty reduces real estate market demand, and falling housing prices may impact household asset values and financial security, affecting both homebuyers and the real estate-related industries. Additionally, rising unemployment and declining income put greater pressure on social security systems, requiring the government to allocate more resources to support the unemployed and low-income families, ensuring basic living standards. The economic challenges, including unemployment, reduced income, and rising living costs, lead to increased psychological stress among the population, severely impacting personal quality of life and well-being.

9.3 Contemporary Revelations

The asteroid impact is one of the most catastrophic events in Earth's history, with profound and lasting impacts on the biosphere. This event altered Earth's climate and environment, directly leading to the extinction of dinosaurs. Dinosaurs, once the dominant species on Earth, were characterized by their large size and powerful survival abilities, occupying the top of the food chain during the Cretaceous period. However, the asteroid impact during the Cambrian period completely overturned this dominance, turning the dinosaurs' strengths into fatal weaknesses almost instantaneously.

Before the asteroid impact, dinosaurs, due to their massive size and powerful predatory abilities, were the rulers of Earth. Their enormous size meant they had few natural predators, and their strong bodies and various adaptive traits allowed them to occupy the highest position in the ecosystem. Dinosaurs were not only effective hunters but also foraged in lush vegetation, providing enough energy for their massive bodies.

However, this size advantage became a fatal flaw after the asteroid impact. The impact triggered drastic environmental changes, shrouding Earth's surface in dust and smoke. This dust blocked sunlight, causing global temperatures to plummet. At this point, Earth's ecosystem underwent a dramatic transformation—plants could no longer perform photosynthesis, leading to widespread plant death, which subsequently affected plant-eating animals.

In this environmental shift, the dinosaurs' massive size became their Achilles' heel. Their large bodies required vast amounts of food, especially plant-based food, to sustain themselves. However, as plant resources dwindled, dinosaurs could not obtain enough food, leading to starvation and a survival crisis. In contrast, smaller animals, with their smaller bodies and lower food requirements, could survive on less food. Their survival flexibility and adaptability allowed them to endure this period of food scarcity.

This shift highlights the relativity of "size." In a stable environment, the large size of dinosaurs was undoubtedly an advantage, but in extreme conditions, this advantage could turn into a disadvantage. The large size of dinosaurs during the end-Cretaceous environmental upheaval meant they faced severe survival challenges, ultimately leading to their extinction.

9.4 Is Bigger Always Better?

The story of dinosaur extinction raises an important question: Is bigger always better? From the extinction of dinosaurs, we can see that being large does not always equate to being advantageous; rather, it is relative. In the face of drastic environmental changes, large size not only fails to provide an advantage but can also become a survival obstacle. The dinosaurs' large size required vast resources, and when environmental changes led to resource depletion, this enormous demand became a burden.

Did dinosaurs become Earth's rulers by actively adapting to their environment, or did they go extinct because they resisted change? The extinction of dinosaurs was more due to rapid environmental changes, and dinosaurs lacked the flexibility and adaptability to cope with such changes. When faced with sudden environmental shifts, dinosaurs exhibited significant passivity, while the real change was in the environment, which filtered out the species.

The extinction of dinosaurs exemplifies the idea that "what makes you strong can also make you weak." During times of abundant food supply on Earth, the large size of dinosaurs was undoubtedly an advantage in the existing environment, but in the new environment, it became a fatal burden. This demonstrates that in an ever-changing natural environment, success does not solely depend on inherent traits but also on the ability to adapt to environmental changes. The extinction of dinosaurs was not only a challenge to their survival abilities but also a severe test of their adaptability to environmental changes (Fig. 9.3).

Ultimately, environmental changes determined the survival and extinction of species. The large size of dinosaurs, unable to adapt to the new environmental conditions, became the reason for their extinction. The story of dinosaurs serves as a valuable lesson for entrepreneurs: when faced with change, flexibility, and adaptability may often be more important than sheer strength and size.

Fig. 9.3 Bigger is not always better; sometimes being small and specialized is more advantageous than being large and strong. The environment ultimately determines which is better

References

1. A. A. Chiarenza, A. Farnsworth, P. D. Mannion, et al., "Asteroid Impact, Not Volcanism, Caused the End-Cretaceous Dinosaur Extinction," Proceedings of the National Academy of Sciences of the United States of America, vol. 117, no. 29, pp. 17084–17093, 2020.
2. D. M. Raup and J. J. Sepkoski Jr, "Mass Extinctions in the Marine Fossil Record," Science, vol. 215, no. 4539, pp. 1501–1503, 1982.
3. L. W. Alvarez, W. Alvarez, F. Asaro, et al., "Extraterrestrial Cause for the

Cretaceous-Tertiary Extinction," Science, vol. 208, no. 4448, pp. 1095–1108, 1980.

4. S. L. Brusatte, R. J. Butler, P. M. Barrett, et al., "The Extinction of the Dinosaurs," Biological Reviews, vol. 90, no. 2, pp. 628–642, 2015.
5. A. A. Chiarenza, A. Farnsworth, P. D. Mannion, et al., "Asteroid Impact, Not Volcanism, Caused the End-Cretaceous Dinosaur Extinction," Proceedings of the National Academy of Sciences, vol. 117, no. 29, pp. 1708–17093, 2020.
6. S. D'Hondt, "Consequences of the Cretaceous/Paleogene Mass Extinction for Marine Ecosystems," Annual Review of Ecology, Evolution, and Systematics, vol. 36, no. 1, pp. 295–317, 2005.
7. M. J. Benton, Vertebrate Palaeontology, John Wiley & Sons, 2014.
8. W. B. Gallagher, "Selective Extinction and Survival Across the Cretaceous/Tertiary Boundary in the Northern Atlantic Coastal Plain," Geology, vol. 19, no. 10, pp. 967–970, 1991.
9. G. Keller, W. Stinnesbeck, T. Adatte, et al., "Multiple Impacts Across the Cretaceous–Tertiary Boundary," Earth-Science Review, vol. 62, no. 3–4, pp. 327–363, 2003.
10. D. E. Fastovsky and D. B. Weishampel, The Evolution and Extinction of the Dinosaurs. Cambridge University Press, 2005.
11. D. Jablonski, "Survival Without Recovery After Mass Extinctions," Proceedings of the National Academy of Sciences of the United States of America, vol. 99, no. 12, pp. 8139–8144, 2002.

CHAPTER 10

The Boundaries of AI Capabilities

10.1 Is AI Omnipotent or Limited?

The development of artificial intelligence (AI) technology has significantly transformed the way industries operate. From automation in manufacturing to diagnostic support systems in healthcare, AI applications are enhancing efficiency and reducing costs. However, this rapid development has also sparked concerns about the future role of humans as AI increasingly takes over tasks once performed by people. These concerns are justified, as history shows that the introduction and widespread adoption of new technologies often lead to profound social changes. For example, during the Industrial Revolution, machines replaced many manual labor jobs, leading to widespread unemployment and social unrest. Today, as AI begins to take over jobs that require high intelligence, such as legal analysis, financial trading, and even journalism, there are fears that these changes could bring about similar or even more severe social problems.

Despite the broad prospects for AI applications, we must not overlook its current limitations. In terms of creativity, while AI can generate art, music, and text, these creations are usually based on existing data combinations and pattern recognition rather than true creative thinking. AI lacks personal experience, emotions, and cultural background, making it incapable of genuine originality. For example, AI-generated artworks may be technically impressive but often lack the deep emotional and meaningful layers found in human art. In terms of emotional understanding,

X. Cao, *Modern Business Management*,
https://doi.org/10.1007/978-981-96-0594-1_10

AI systems can recognize and analyze emotional expressions (such as through sentiment analysis), but they cannot truly understand or experience emotions. This limits AI's effectiveness in applications requiring deep emotional insight, such as psychological counseling or interpersonal relationship management. In terms of common sense reasoning, AI often struggles with tasks requiring common sense. Common sense is basic knowledge and understanding gained through human life experience, and AI systems, without explicit data, find it difficult to perform reasonable common sense reasoning. For example, AI might have trouble understanding sarcasm, metaphors, or culturally embedded implicit meanings in conversation. In terms of complex decision-making, AI still finds it challenging to handle decisions involving multiple variables and uncertainties. Although AI can optimize specific objective functions, its performance may fall short when faced with decisions that require comprehensive consideration of ethical, social, and environmental factors. For instance, in healthcare, AI may excel in diagnosis but face challenges in formulating comprehensive treatment plans that consider individual patient differences and lifestyles. In terms of adaptability, current AI systems usually perform well within a specific range of training data but may see a significant drop in performance when encountering entirely new, unseen situations. For example, a well-trained image recognition model might fail to accurately identify objects not included in the training set. In handling uncertainty, AI's performance is still limited. Many AI systems rely on deterministic algorithms and preset rules, and when dealing with ambiguous or incomplete information, AI may struggle to make reasonable judgments. This is particularly evident in real-time data analysis and dynamic environments, such as the performance of autonomous vehicles in extreme weather conditions. In ethical decision-making, AI systems currently cannot perform complex ethical and moral judgments. Although algorithms can model specific ethical issues, they cannot truly understand the complexity of ethics and values in human society. For example, the decision-making process in an autonomous vehicle during an accident, aimed at minimizing harm, involves complex ethical considerations that current AI systems find difficult to handle satisfactorily. In terms of law and social norms, AI also faces challenges in following and adapting to laws and social norms. While AI can be designed to comply with established rules, it may lack a deep understanding of the societal values underlying these laws when interpreting and applying legal provisions. Regarding computing resources, training large AI models, such as deep learning models, typically requires vast amounts of computing resources, including high-performance computing chips and large-scale data centers. These resource demands make AI applications expensive, limiting their widespread adoption in some fields. In terms of energy consumption, training and running complex AI models consume significant amounts of energy, impacting the environment. As AI models become increasingly complex, the issue of energy consumption becomes more severe, raising challenges in sustainability and environmental protection. In terms of security, AI systems may become targets of cyberattacks, especially in applications involving sensitive data and critical infrastructure. For example, vulnerabilities in AI systems could be exploited by hackers, leading to data breaches or system failures. Regarding adversarial attacks, AI models are vulnerable to adversarial attacks, where carefully crafted input data perturbs the model's predictions. Such attacks can lead to incorrect judgments by AI systems, posing threats to security and reliability.

Despite the many limitations of current AI, we cannot ignore its future potential. From the perspective of human history, all activities reliant on intelligence could gradually be replaced by AI. However, this process is not instantaneous but rather gradual. During this process, human society needs to take appropriate measures to mitigate potential shocks (Fig. 10.1).

First, we need to manage and oversee the development of AI reasonably to ensure its applications do not cause irreversible negative impacts on society. This includes establishing relevant laws and regulations to ensure AI's transparency and explainability while limiting its application scope to avoid misuse. Second, we should explore models of human-AI collaborative development. Even though AI can perform more and more tasks, humans still hold irreplaceable advantages in creative thinking, moral judgment, and complex interpersonal relationship management. By cultivating the ability to collaborate with AI, humans can use it as a tool to enhance productivity and creativity rather than becoming competitors. Finally, as AI technology becomes more widespread, we need to raise public awareness and education about AI at the societal level. Educating the public about AI's strengths and limitations can reduce panic and misunderstandings, better preparing society to face the challenges brought by this technological transformation.

The rapid development of AI indeed brings many concerns and anxieties, especially regarding its potential impact on social structures and

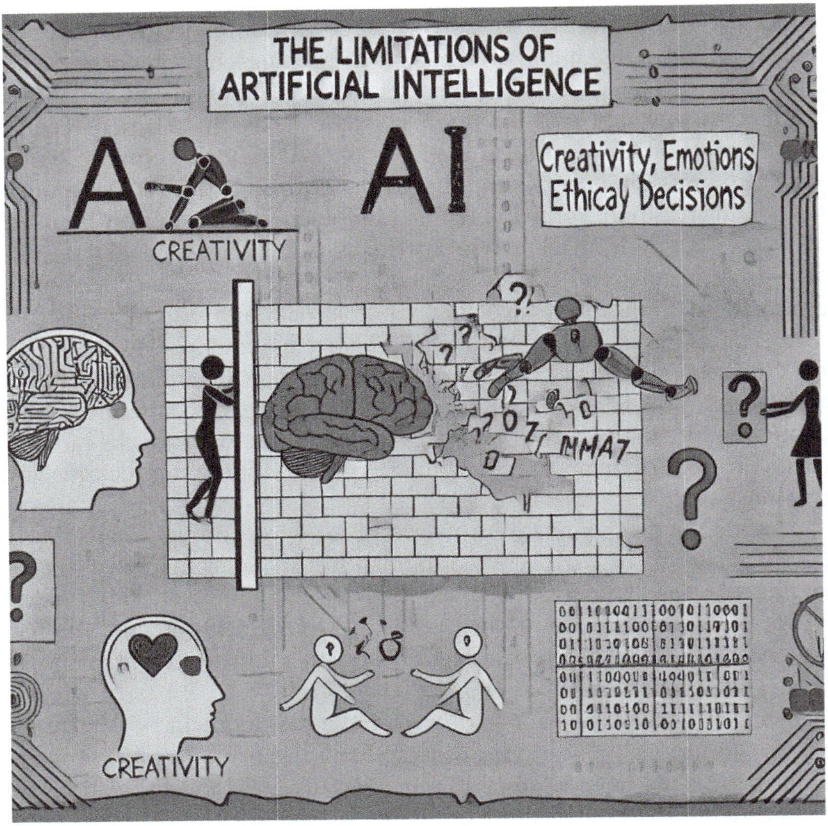

Fig. 10.1 AI has many limitations

employment patterns. However, as discussed, current AI still has significant limitations that will persist in the short term. By understanding and managing these limitations, we can better predict future trends and develop corresponding strategies to ensure AI's development brings more benefits than threats to human society.

10.2 Escaping the Risk of Being Replaced by AI

In today's fast-paced AI development environment, entrepreneurs face unprecedented opportunities and challenges. Although AI performs excellently in many fields, its limitations also present unique opportunities for entrepreneurs. Understanding these limitations and using them to guide your business strategy can help you stand out in the fierce market competition and reduce the risk of being replaced by AI.

One notable limitation of AI is its shortcomings in creativity and emotional understanding. While AI can generate seemingly original artworks, music, or texts, these creations often lack true human emotion and cultural context. As an entrepreneur, you can turn this distinction into a competitive advantage. For instance, in fields such as art, design, and branding, human intuition and emotion remain irreplaceable. You can create artworks or designs with a unique personal style and deep emotional connection, resonating with customers and helping you stand out in the market. Additionally, providing high-quality customer service and personalized experiences is another promising direction. Although AI can automate many customer service tasks, it cannot replace human capabilities in establishing deep emotional connections and handling complex emotional issues. Offering personalized consulting services for high-end clients or incorporating deep emotional understanding into psychological counseling and interpersonal relationship management can help you build a unique advantage in these areas.

AI still faces challenges in handling complex decision-making and common sense reasoning. While AI systems can efficiently analyze and optimize within a data range, they often struggle in situations requiring common sense and complex ethical judgment. As an entrepreneur, you can leverage this by offering decision-support tools and services, especially in fields such as healthcare, law, or high-end finance. Decision-making in these fields requires the combination of human experience and professional judgment, with AI mainly providing data analysis and trend prediction. By combining AI's technical strengths with human experts' intuition and experience, you can create more comprehensive and accurate decision-support systems. Additionally, developing education and training services for AI users is a field worth exploring. Training users to understand and address AI's limitations can help them better utilize this technology, enhancing their competitiveness in the market.

AI's reliance on data quality is another clear limitation. The performance of AI systems is directly affected by the quality of the data they are trained on. If the data is biased or insufficient, AI outcomes may be limited. Therefore, offering services such as data cleaning, integration, and annotation can become a business opportunity. By helping companies improve data accuracy and completeness, you can fill a market gap and lay the foundation for successful AI implementation.

Moreover, AI's adaptability issues in dynamic and uncertain environments are significant limitations. Many AI systems perform well under static data conditions but may encounter challenges in changing environments. As an entrepreneur, you can develop adaptable solutions to help companies quickly adjust strategies in constantly changing markets. For example, offering customized AI application services or designing technology solutions that efficiently respond to dynamic environments can help you succeed in this field.

AI's shortcomings in moral and ethical judgment are another important limitation. Although AI can perform basic ethical modeling through algorithms, it lacks a true understanding of complex moral issues. Therefore, offering AI ethics consulting and compliance services is a promising entrepreneurial direction. Helping companies adhere to laws and regulations while addressing ethical issues during AI development and application will not only meet market demand but also ensure the legal and ethical use of technology.

AI technology's high demand for computing resources and energy is a significant limiting factor. As AI models become more complex, the challenges of computing costs and energy consumption become more prominent. As an entrepreneur, you can develop energy-efficient and high-performance AI technology solutions or offer services that optimize computing resource management. By designing more energy-efficient computing hardware, optimizing algorithms, or providing green technology consulting services, you can innovate while contributing to environmental sustainability.

AI systems' security and adversarial challenges are current critical issues. AI models are susceptible to adversarial attacks, which can lead to incorrect judgments by the system. Therefore, developing and offering security solutions for AI systems is a field with broad prospects. Offering advanced firewalls, intrusion detection systems, or adversarial training tools to help companies protect their AI systems from security threats will help establish your market position (Fig. 10.2).

Fig. 10.2 Actively engaging in fields where AI struggles can help avoid the risk of being replaced by AI

In conclusion, while the rapid development of AI technology presents many challenges, its limitations also provide rich opportunities for entrepreneurs. By focusing on areas where AI struggles and offering high-value-added services and solutions, you can find a path to success in this new technological environment. Understanding these limitations and leveraging them will help you create unique competitive advantages in the age of artificial intelligence, driving the successful development of your entrepreneurial ventures.

References

1. S. J. Russell and P. Norvig, Artificial Intelligence: A Modern Approach. Pearson, 2016.
2. K. P. Murphy, Machine Learning: A Probabilistic Perspective. MIT Press, 2012.
3. P. J. Werbos, "Backpropagation Through Time: What It Does and How to Do It," Proceedings of the IEEE, vol. 78, no. 10, pp. 1550–1560, 1990.
4. M. Mitchell, Artificial Intelligence: A Guide for Thinking Humans, 2019.
5. D. Silver, T. Hubert, J. Schrittwieser, et al., "Mastering Chess and Shogi by Self-Play with a General Reinforcement Learning Algorithm," arXiv preprint arXiv:1712.01815, 2017.
6. J. Macqueen, "Some Methods for Classification and Analysis of Multivariate Observations," in Proceedings of the 5th Berkeley Symposium on Mathematical Statistics and Probability. University of California Press, 1967.
7. D. J. C. MacKay, Information Theory, Inference and Learning Algorithms. Cambridge University Press, 2003.
8. Y. LeCun, Y. Bengio, and G. Hinton, "Deep Learning," Nature, vol. 521, no. 7553, pp. 436–444, 2015.
9. L. Cao, "Data science: A comprehensive Overview," ACM Computing Surveys (CSUR), vol. 50, no. 3, pp. 1–42, 2017.
10. G. Hinton, L. Deng, D. Yu, et al., "Deep Neural Networks for Acoustic Modeling in Speech Recognition: The Shared Views of Four Research Groups," IEEE Signal Processing Magazine, vol. 29, no. 6, pp. 82–97, 2012.
11. I. Goodfellow, J. Pouget-Abadie, M. Mirza, et al., "Generative Adversarial Nets," in Advances in Neural Information Processing Systems, vol. 27, 2014.
12. N. Bostrom and E. Yudkowsky, "The Ethics of Artificial Intelligence," in Artificial Intelligence Safety and Security. Chapman and Hall/CRC, 2018, pp. 57–69.

CHAPTER 11

The Evolution from Mental Labor Today to Physical Labor Tomorrow

11.1 The Glory Days of the Past

In the 1980s in China, the profession of driving was highly respected and considered a skill-intensive and honorable job. At that time, driving licenses were not as common as they are today, and obtaining one required a high level of skill and aptitude, with limited driving schools available. Learning to drive involved a significant investment of time and effort to accumulate enough practical experience, as vehicles lacked the intelligent assistance systems of modern cars, demanding higher technical skills and adaptability from drivers when navigating complex road conditions. Becoming a driver not only signified mastering a rare skill but also indicated a relatively high social status. China was in the early stages of economic reform, and private cars were extremely rare, with most drivers working for government departments or large state-owned enterprises. As a result, drivers often had the opportunity to interact with important organizations and leaders, and even participate in high-level social affairs, earning them considerable respect in society. Drivers' income at that time was usually higher than that of ordinary workers. Due to the rarity of driving skills and vehicles, the profession offered a stable and substantial economic return. In addition to basic wages, drivers often received extra allowances, such as travel expenses for long-distance transportation, making their living conditions relatively superior. In the social structure of the time, the stability of the driving profession was also

X. Cao, *Modern Business Management*,
https://doi.org/10.1007/978-981-96-0594-1_11

highly valued. In the 1980s, job distribution in China was relatively fixed, and becoming a driver meant securing a "job for life," especially when working for government agencies or state-owned enterprises, providing continuity and security. Compared to other manual labor jobs, driving was seen as a more relaxed and secure occupation, thus considered an ideal profession. Additionally, drivers were seen as symbols of possessing rare skills. Due to the relatively underdeveloped transportation infrastructure, drivers needed not only to drive proficiently but also to understand vehicle maintenance and repair, making them regarded as "all-round" talents. In some special units, such as the military or police departments, drivers needed not only to operate vehicles but also to perform emergency tasks, enhancing their sense of professional honor.

There was a widespread consensus that driving was not just manual labor but also required mental labor. The profession demanded a range of skills and abilities to handle the various challenges encountered in daily work. During driving, drivers needed to maintain a high level of attention, especially in complex traffic environments. They had to constantly observe road conditions, recognize road signs, traffic lights, pedestrians, and the movements of other vehicles, and react quickly. This demand for concentration was not just short term but persisted throughout the driving process, especially on long-distance trips, where drivers needed to stay alert for extended periods to avoid accidents caused by fatigue. Drivers often had to make split-second decisions during driving. For instance, in an emergency, they needed to quickly judge how to avoid obstacles or choose the safest driving route. These decisions had to be both fast and accurate, directly impacting the safety of passengers and other road users. Moreover, when faced with traffic jams, adverse weather conditions, or sudden mechanical failures, drivers needed to respond flexibly and develop the best driving plan, testing their adaptability and decision-making skills. Although today's drivers can rely on navigation systems, in the past, and in some complex or low-signal environments even now, drivers needed a good sense of direction and route planning skills. They had to be familiar with the city's road network and even remember less frequently used alternative routes to handle sudden traffic congestion or road closures. Especially in long-distance transportation, drivers needed to master the main traffic routes nationwide, understand the traffic characteristics of different sections, and choose the best driving route based on weather and road conditions (Fig. 11.1).

Fig. 11.1 The profession of driving had a certain technical threshold and was once widely regarded as a skill-intensive occupation

Driving often involved high-intensity pressure, such as completing transportation tasks within tight deadlines or driving in adverse weather conditions. In these situations, drivers needed to maintain good psychological resilience, stay calm under pressure, and make reasonable judgments. They also had to manage the psychological fatigue associated with long periods of driving, especially in long-distance transportation, where maintaining mental balance and stability was key to safe driving. The job often required communication with multiple roles, such as dispatchers, customers, and traffic management personnel. Drivers needed to flexibly use communication skills when interacting with different people to ensure accurate information transmission and smooth workflow. They also had to coordinate various interests, such as scheduling loading and unloading times in freight transportation, ensuring the goods were delivered safely and on time, and testing their coordination and organizational abilities. Early drivers not only needed to drive but also had to possess some mechanical knowledge to deal with potential vehicle breakdowns during travel. They had to know how to perform basic vehicle inspections and repairs, assess whether the vehicle was in good working condition, and take necessary measures in emergencies to ensure driving safety. In certain industries, such as hazardous materials transportation or specialized vehicle operation, drivers needed to master specific professional knowledge, such as how to safely transport dangerous goods or operate additional equipment on specialized vehicles. These tasks went beyond simple driving and required complex mental labor.

In summary, driving relied not only on physical operational skills but also required significant mental labor. The profession demanded high concentration, complex decision-making skills, route planning abilities, psychological resilience, communication and coordination skills, as well as professional knowledge and expertise. It was this combination of mental and technical skills that made driving far more than just manual labor—it was a job requiring high intelligence and high-skill levels.

11.2 The Rise of Autonomous Driving and the Decline of the Driving Profession

The emergence of autonomous driving technology, particularly the widespread adoption of autonomous taxis, poses an unprecedented challenge to the traditional driving profession. The rapid development and application of this technology have not only questioned the threshold of the driving profession but also triggered deep reflections on the future of job structures. Let's start with a simple comparison to examine the differences between autonomous driving and human driving from various perspectives (Fig. 11.2).

Traditional manual driving relies on the driver's experience, intuition, and flexible adaptability. Drivers can make instant decisions in complex and uncertain situations, handling various emergencies such as sudden obstacles on the road, unexpected pedestrian crossings, or driving in

Fig. 11.2 The advent of autonomous driving poses a serious threat to the driving profession. Public perception of the driving industry is also undergoing significant changes, with the technical threshold of driving increasingly seen as low, and the profession more as low-skill manual labor

adverse weather conditions. However, autonomous driving technology, through advanced sensors, artificial intelligence, and data processing capabilities, gradually compensates for the shortcomings of traditional driving. For example, autonomous driving systems can monitor and analyze the surrounding environment in real-time around the clock, avoiding accidents caused by human fatigue or distraction. As the technology matures, autonomous driving is even safer and more efficient than human driving in many cases.

Hiring drivers involves high labor costs, including wages, insurance, and benefits. Additionally, human driving may lead to unstable driving quality due to personal factors (such as fatigue or emotional fluctuations), affecting efficiency and safety. The emergence of autonomous taxis significantly reduces operating costs. Once the initial investment in an autonomous fleet is recovered, there is no need to pay drivers' wages and benefits, and the operating and maintenance costs are significantly lower than for human-driven vehicles. For consumers, this means lower travel costs, giving autonomous taxis a competitive advantage in the market.

Driving as a profession with a high technical threshold requires professional training and long-term experience accumulation to master complex driving skills and adaptability. This high threshold has historically ensured the important status of drivers in society. The core of autonomous driving technology lies in algorithms, sensors, and data processing. It depends on technological development rather than individual skills and experience. This means that the professional skills of traditional drivers are no longer irreplaceable in the face of autonomous driving. In fact, the technical threshold of driving has shifted from manual driving skills to the development, maintenance, and management of autonomous driving systems.

In the past, drivers were respected for their technical skills and sense of responsibility, especially in positions requiring advanced driving techniques. However, with the rise of autonomous driving technology, the social status of this profession is gradually being eroded. People are beginning to question whether human driving is still worth high regard, given that machines can perform driving tasks more safely and efficiently.

The widespread adoption of autonomous driving may lead to mass unemployment or pressure for career transitions among drivers. Society will need to redefine the value of the driving profession and help those who once relied on it for a living find new employment opportunities. Driving was once a skill-intensive and honorable profession. People took pride in being able to perform driving tasks, especially when demonstrating superior skills in complex and challenging driving environments. The emergence of autonomous driving challenges this professional pride. Machines can surpass human drivers in many ways, particularly in terms of safety and efficiency. This has led to reflections on whether driving is truly a high-skill, high-threshold job or a task that machines can easily replace.

By comparing the above points, we can conclude that the threshold of the profession has shifted. The rise of autonomous driving technology indicates that the traditional high-threshold driving profession is undergoing fundamental changes. In the past, the threshold for the driving profession lay in driving skills and adaptability; now, the threshold has shifted to the development and management of autonomous driving systems. This comparison reveals how technological progress redefines professional thresholds and prompts deep reflections on the future direction of career development. In this context, traditional driving skills may no longer symbolize a high threshold, but new technical fields have created new high-threshold professions. Although early on, people did not consider driving to be mental labor, it was widely believed to be a high-tech occupation, certainly not purely manual labor. However, with the widespread adoption of autonomous driving and various automotive sensors and intelligent accessories, the driving profession has gradually degraded into pure manual labor, a consensus increasingly accepted by the public.

11.3 Is Programming Still Attractive?

Over the past few decades, the profession of computer programming has undergone significant changes. Once upon a time, programmers were seen as highly paid and technically demanding mental laborers. Programming work was full of complexity and creativity, and many considered it a high-value profession. However, over time, society's perception of this profession has started to change, with more and more people believing that programming work has gradually become more process-driven and standardized, even approaching manual labor. This shift has deep underlying reasons and impacts (Fig. 11.3).

Firstly, the standardization and tooling of programming is a key factor. With the increasing maturity of programming languages and development frameworks, many programming tasks have become more standardized and modular. For example, the widespread use of the Java language in enterprise development has made much of the programmers' work highly repetitive. They no longer need to write complex algorithms or design new system architectures from scratch but instead assemble code

Fig. 11.3 Programmers are gradually shifting from white-collar mental labor to what some call "IT laborers" engaged in manual labor

according to established patterns by calling existing libraries and frameworks. Additionally, the proliferation of code generation tools, integrated development environments (IDEs), and automated testing tools has made programming work more process-driven and mechanical. These tools help programmers quickly complete tasks that once required significant time and mental effort, thereby reducing the creativity and technical content of the work.

Secondly, the rapid spread of training and education has lowered the entry threshold for this industry. In the past, becoming a programmer usually required systematic learning through higher education in computer science. Now, more and more people can qualify for entry-level development work through a few months of training courses. These courses aim to quickly produce "coders" capable of performing basic development tasks required by businesses using existing tools and frameworks, without needing a deep understanding of underlying principles or algorithm design. As a result, the entry threshold for the programming industry has become lower, attracting a large number of newcomers, and further accelerating the process-driven nature of this profession.

Moreover, the nature of programmers' work has subtly changed. In large software development projects, many programmers focus mainly on developing or maintaining specific modules, often involving highly repetitive tasks akin to assembly line work. They need to complete tasks according to established norms and standards rather than engage in independent innovation or design. As software development has become more globalized and outsourced, programming tasks have been divided into smaller, simpler parts and distributed among different teams or individuals. This division of labor further reduces the need for individual programmers to engage in creative work, making them more executors of predetermined tasks than performers of highly challenging intellectual work.

This transformation is also reflected in social perception. The term "coder," with its somewhat derogatory connotation, has become increasingly popular, suggesting that programming work is similar to traditional manual labor, requiring a lot of repetitive physical effort rather than creative mental work. Once, the work of a programmer was considered a symbol of high technology and high value, with relatively strong professional pride. However, as the industry changes, the social status and self-esteem of programmers, particularly in highly repetitive roles, are gradually being challenged, leading them to increasingly feel the "laborization" of their work.

Changes in market demand and salary structures further exacerbate this trend. With the layering and standardization of programming work, the salary structure of programmers has also changed. Top-tier programmers, especially those working in cutting-edge technology areas such as artificial intelligence (AI) and big data, still enjoy high salaries and status. However, the salaries of many programmers engaged in basic development work, especially in outsourced or entry-level positions, have gradually become ordinary, failing to match the high income once associated with the profession. At the same time, as more people enter the programming industry, market competition intensifies, leading to an oversupply of basic programmers, reducing their bargaining power in the market and further diminishing the attractiveness and perceived value of the profession.

Looking to the future, the career prospects of programmers face new challenges. With the development of automation tools and artificial intelligence, more programming tasks may be automated in the future. This means that the nature of the programming profession may further shift toward manual labor unless programmers can master more advanced skills such as algorithm design, system architecture, and AI model development. In this context, programmers need to continuously learn and adapt to new technologies to avoid being left behind by industry changes. Those who can enhance their skills and engage in higher-level technical development will continue to maintain their status as mental laborers, while those who cannot keep up with technological advancements may be forced to transition or face career crises.

The changing nature of the computer programming profession reflects the dual influence of technological progress and social perception. Although programming still involves many complex intellectual tasks, with the advancement of process-driven and standardized approaches, certain aspects of the programmer profession are gradually aligning with manual labor. This change reminds us that in the context of ongoing technological evolution, the nature and value of professions are not static but dynamically adjust over time and in response to societal needs.

11.4 Re-assessing: Today's Mental Labor Degrades into Tomorrow's Physical Labor

This leads us to reassess industries that were once firmly believed to be "manual labor." With the driving profession under threat from autonomous driving, many believe it is only a matter of time before drivers are replaced by robots, as driving is perceived as a low-threshold, low-skill, simple, and repetitive manual task. Due to the lack of a technical threshold, replacement by machines seems inevitable. However, little did they know that thirty years ago, in the 1990s, learning to drive required attending specialized training schools and undergoing full-time, long-term study. At that time, driving was considered a highly technical profession. Similarly, operating machine tools was a hot job decades ago because people firmly believed that this technical occupation had a high threshold and was difficult to replace. However, contrary to expectations, with the proliferation of CNC (computer numerical control) machine tools, people gradually accepted the notion that operating a machine tool has a low threshold and that CNC machines replaced manual operators because it was purely manual labor with no core technical threshold—just a process to follow. How similar is this process? (Fig. 11.4).

Looking back a hundred years ago, wasn't Rickshaw Boy pulling a rickshaw similar to today's car driver? Perhaps, in comparison, driving a car may even seem more technically demanding. In reality, a hundred

Fig. 11.4 Today's mental labor gradually degrades into tomorrow's physical labor

years ago, a good rickshaw puller needed to know the city's roads well, requiring a good memory; they needed to quickly plan the shortest route to the customer's destination, requiring good intelligence; and they had to precisely navigate the rickshaw over uneven surfaces to avoid bumps, requiring high-efficiency handling skills. In the context of the time, wouldn't this be considered a high-threshold technical job? Could it be considered mental labor? Yet today, no one considers it to have had any technical threshold.

In fact, the process of technological development is about gradually turning what was once considered mental labor into manual labor, thereby creating mental labor at a higher level and dimension. There is no eternal mental labor, only temporary mental labor. The era when mastering a skill could last a lifetime is gone forever.

References

1. D. J. C. MacKay, Information Theory, Inference and Learning Algorithms. Cambridge University Press, 2003.
2. J. MacQueen, "Some Methods for Classification and Analysis of Multivariate Observations," Proceedings of the 5th Berkeley Symposium on Mathematical Statistics and Probability, University of California Press, 1967.
3. N. Bostrom and E. Yudkowsky, The Ethics of Artificial Intelligence, in Artificial Intelligence Safety and Security. Chapman and Hall/CRC, 2018, pp. 57–69.
4. L. Cao, "Data Science: A Comprehensive Overview," ACM Computing Surveys (CSUR), vol. 50, no. 3, pp. 1–42, 2017.
5. A. Creswell, T. White, V. Dumoulin, and others, "Generative Adversarial Networks: An Overview," IEEE Signal Processing Magazine, vol. 35, no. 1, pp. 53–65, 2018.
6. K. P. Murphy, Probabilistic Machine Learning: An Introduction. MIT Press, 2022.
7. Y. Bengio, I. Goodfellow, and A. Courville, Deep Learning. MIT Press, Cambridge, MA, USA, 2017.
8. R. A. Kowalski, "Artificial Intelligence and Human Thinking," in Twenty-Second International Joint Conference on Artificial Intelligence, 2011.

CHAPTER 12

One Step Ahead Is a Pioneer, Two Steps Ahead Is a Martyr

12.1 Disproportionate Contribution and Reward

In recent years, artificial intelligence (AI) has experienced explosive growth, rapidly rising to become the darling of the capital markets. Investors worldwide have flocked to AI-related projects, hoping to secure a place in this technological revolution. For example, technologies based on recommendation systems, such as news, video, and product recommendations, have attracted substantial investments due to their enormous market potential and rapidly growing user demand. According to statistics, the global AI market reached nearly $327.5 billion in 2022, and it is expected to continue growing at a double-digit rate in the coming years.

In specific fields, such as facial recognition, image recognition, voice recognition, and robotics, startups have flourished and quickly expanded their markets. Many companies have successfully gone public and become new unicorns. For instance, China's Megvii (Face ++) secured $750 million in funding in 2019 and went public in 2021. Similarly, leading companies in image recognition technology, like Yitu Technology, have also gained favor in the capital markets. These companies have leveraged AI technology to find opportunities in various industries, rapidly transforming sectors from financial services to healthcare and public safety.

However, while AI has soared, the once-promising 5G technology has followed a different trajectory. In 2022 and 2023, 5G was heralded as a

X. Cao, *Modern Business Management*,
https://doi.org/10.1007/978-981-96-0594-1_12

crucial milestone for future technological development, expected to revolutionize our lifestyles and work environments by enabling faster data transmission speeds and lower latency, thereby driving advancements in autonomous driving, the Internet of Things (IoT), and smart cities. Many anticipated that 5G would lead to a technological revolution, making society smarter and more efficient. Yet by 2024, the enthusiasm for 5G had waned. Although some sectors have benefited, overall, 5G has not lived up to its initial high expectations. This phenomenon has led to reflections on whether 5G truly possesses the transformative power it once promised.

In comparing AI and 5G, many may overestimate the value of AI while underestimating the significance of 5G. Take facial recognition technology, for example: although it is widely used in everyday life, such as in airport security checks and smartphone unlocking, the core technology behind it was developed many years ago. High-precision facial recognition relies on deep learning algorithms, which succeed due to extensive data training. The data needed to train these algorithms comes from billions of cameras and sensors, whose widespread adoption was made possible by the significant reduction in hardware costs and advances in storage technology over the past few decades.

Consider a practical example: around the year 2000, digital cameras were still very expensive, with a typical camera costing thousands of dollars, and storage devices had very limited capacity. However, by 2020, the performance of smartphone cameras had improved dramatically, and costs had plummeted. These breakthroughs in hardware, particularly the reduced cost of cameras and storage devices, laid a solid foundation for subsequent AI applications.

A similar situation is evident in the chip industry. Today, many AI technologies rely on high-performance devices like graphics processing units (GPUs). These devices can process massive amounts of data and perform complex calculations quickly to support AI algorithms. Companies like Nvidia have reaped huge commercial successes from this demand, with their market value surpassing a trillion dollars in 2023. However, this success would not have been possible without decades of accumulation in the semiconductor industry, including advances in chip design and manufacturing processes. In other words, AI's development is built on the progress of traditional technologies like chips, storage devices, and network infrastructure (Fig. 12.1).

Fig. 12.1 Those who deliver the final "kick" often reap the greatest rewards, while those who laid the foundation may not receive the recognition or rewards they deserve from the market

From a broader perspective, this reflects a general societal phenomenon: people tend to reward those who deliver the final successful push, while often overlooking those who laid the groundwork for that success. For example, when we gain admission to a university, we often thank our high school teachers, especially our homeroom teacher, for their crucial guidance as we neared the college entrance exams. However, we tend to overlook the elementary and middle school teachers who provided our foundational education. Similarly, while electronic engineering and computer science are widely recognized as the driving forces behind the development of the internet, the important contributions of fiber-optic cable and communication materials researchers are often ignored. Likewise, in the development of AI and autonomous driving technologies, while AI algorithms are seen as the core, we must not overlook the fundamental role of hardware infrastructure, particularly motor and sensor technology, in enabling autonomous vehicles.

From a government perspective, these examples remind us that in the wave of technological development, we should not only focus on those who deliver the final innovations but also recognize the importance of long-term accumulation. Future technological advancements and commercial success will depend on continued investment in and improvement of infrastructure. Only then can we truly achieve technological transformation and drive societal progress. However, from an individual perspective, these examples suggest that we should rationally pursue becoming the "final innovator" to reap the rewards of the times.

12.2 Entrepreneurial Choices: When All Is Ready, All That's Missing Is the Final Push

In the process of technological innovation and business operations, choosing the right timing and field is crucial for maximizing benefits. We can draw important lessons from the development of AI and 5G technologies. The key takeaway is that when "all is ready, all that's missing is the final push," if you happen to be the one who delivers that push, you will reap the greatest rewards, even taking shares that should belong to others.

Insight 1: Timing is Everything

The timing of a venture determines the ratio of investment to return. If a project has not yet reached the stage where "all is ready, all that's missing is the final push," and is still lacking many core elements, blindly entering the market may lead to high costs and long payback periods. This is because in the early stages of a project, the infrastructure, market demand, and technological maturity may all be insufficient. Investors entering at this stage must pour in significant resources and face a long wait with uncertainty, shouldering the responsibility of building the infrastructure and educating the market. For example, in the early stages of the AI field, when infrastructure like chips, storage, and data acquisition were not yet developed, companies entering the field had to spend substantial resources to develop and perfect these foundational elements, taking on significant risk and pressure.

Take Tesla as another example. Although Tesla has now achieved great success in the electric vehicle industry, in its early days, it had to bear the burden of investing in battery technology development, building charging networks, and other infrastructure—an extremely challenging process. While Tesla succeeded, if too many companies had entered the market when the infrastructure was immature, many would likely have failed due to the high costs and time investment required (Fig. 12.2).

Insight 2: Choosing the Right Field

Choosing the "final push" field when all is ready, rather than a field that is already part of the established elements, ensures that you bring unique value. When the market, technology, and demand have all taken shape, the "final push" often represents a key innovation point that can propel the market to its breakthrough moment. Companies entering the market at this stage can leverage this crucial element to rapidly achieve market breakthroughs and capture significant market share. For example, Apple's launch of the iPhone is an excellent case in point. Before the iPhone, touch screen technology, mobile internet, and the smartphone market had already developed to some extent, but these technologies lacked a product that could truly integrate and elevate the user experience. Apple, with its design and integration capabilities, became the one to deliver the "final push," redefining the smartphone market and reaping substantial market rewards.

In contrast, while 5G technology garnered significant attention in 2022–2023, it appeared to lose momentum in 2024 because its "final push" timing had not fully matured. Although 5G's speed and low latency characteristics offer potential in fields like IoT and smart manufacturing, the corresponding application scenarios and market demand had not fully materialized. Many companies that positioned themselves early in the 5G field, attempting to gain an advantage, faced high upfront investments and lower short-term returns. In contrast, companies that entered

Fig. 12.2 The best time to enter is when all is ready and only the final push is needed

the 5G field when the application scenarios were mature and the technology ecosystem was complete may achieve greater returns due to the momentum provided by the "final push."

Choosing the right timing and field is crucial to winning in the competitive landscape of technology and markets. When the infrastructure and market conditions are in place, and only a key breakthrough is needed, those who seize the "final push" will gain the most significant benefits. Therefore, when making decisions, businesses and investors should avoid entering too early when infrastructure is incomplete, and market demand is unclear. Instead, they should focus on fields that are nearing maturity and only need a critical innovation to drive overall development. This approach maximizes their advantages and yields substantial returns.

References

1. J. Schmidhuber, "Deep Learning in Neural Networks: An Overview," Neural Networks, vol. 61, pp. 85–117, Jan. 2015.
2. P. H. Winston, Artificial Intelligence. Addison-Wesley Longman Publishing Co., Inc., 1992.
3. S. J. Russell and P. Norvig, Artificial Intelligence: A Modern Approach. Pearson, 2016.
4. I. F. Akyildiz, S. Nie, S. C. Lin, et al., "5G Roadmap: 10 Key Enabling Technologies," Computer Networks, vol. 106, pp. 17–48, 2016.
5. J. A. Manner, Spectrum Wars: The Rise of 5G and Beyond. Artech House, 2021.
6. U. Shrivastava and J. K. Verma, "A Study on 5G Technology and Its Applications in Telecommunications," in 2021 International Conference on Computational Performance Evaluation (ComPE), IEEE, 2021, pp. 365–371.
7. J. L. Hennessy, and D. A. Patterson, Computer Architecture: A Quantitative Approach. Morgan Kaufmann, 2017.
8. W. J. Dally, S. W. Keckler, and D. B. Kirk, "Evolution of the Graphics Processing Unit (GPU)," IEEE Micro, vol. 41, no. 6, pp. 42–51, 2021.
9. C. De Luca, B. Lippmann, W. Schober, et al., "AI in Semiconductor Industry," in Artificial Intelligence for Digitising Industry–Applications, River Publishers, 2022, pp. 105–112.
10. E. Ernst, R. Merola, and D. Samaan, "Economics of Artificial Intelligence: Implications for the Future of Work," IZA Journal of Labor Policy, vol. 9, no. 1, 2019.
11. E. Brynjolfsson and A. McAfee, The Second Machine Age: Work, Progress, and Prosperity in a Time of Brilliant Technologies. W. W. Norton & Company, 2014.
12. A. Banerjee and E. Duflo, "Poor Economics: A Radical Rethinking of the Way to Fight Global Poverty," Society and Economy, vol. 35, no. 4, pp. 573–587, 2013.
13. C. M. Christensen, The Innovator's Dilemma: When New Technologies Cause Great Firms to Fail. Harvard Business Review Press, 2015.

14. M. E. Porter and J. E. Heppelmann, "How Smart, Connected Products Are Transforming Competition," Harvard Business Review, vol. 92, no. 11, pp. 64–88, 2014.

CHAPTER 13

A Makeshift Troupe Performing a Grand Opera: The Startup Path of Emerging Companies

13.1 The World as a Makeshift Troupe

The term "makeshift theater" originates from traditional opera troupes and refers to small, temporary theater groups that lack a fixed performance venue. When applied to companies, it suggests significant internal shortcomings such as poor management, inefficient resource allocation, and inadequate innovation capabilities. In 2023, the phrase "the world is a huge makeshift theater" became popular online, reflecting a widespread shift in social sentiment and mindset, particularly resonating with the younger generation (Fig. 13.1).

This phrase highlights broad skepticism about societal mechanisms. People observe that what should be professional and meticulous institutions and systems often appear haphazard and superficial. The metaphor indicates that behind many seemingly grand decisions and systems, the actual operations are chaotic and uncertain. This disillusionment arises from the gap between expectations and reality, especially when people find that the world operates far from the serious and efficient ideal they had envisioned.

Additionally, this mindset leads to a process of "disenchantment." As people realize that the world does not meet their expectations, they gradually lose trust in authority and institutions. This sense of disillusionment is not merely a harsh acknowledgment of reality but also a rejection of

X. Cao, *Modern Business Management*,
https://doi.org/10.1007/978-981-96-0594-1_13

Fig. 13.1 The world is a giant makeshift troupe

previously held ideals. However, this disillusionment is not entirely negative. It encourages people to reassess their expectations of the world, shift toward more practical and independent thinking, and provides an opportunity for personal awakening, stimulating greater autonomy and creativity.

While "the world is a makeshift theater" may sound cynical, it reflects a profound shift in contemporary society—from reliance on external authority and institutions to valuing independent thought and action.

This shift helps us move away from blind admiration for iconic companies, experts, and celebrities, leading to a more rational examination of the world's true nature.

13.2 Imperfection in the Early Stages Is the Norm

The saying "Rome wasn't built in a day" also applies to business development. Successful companies, like complex systems, require time and gradual development. In the early stages, businesses may face many imperfections and immaturities, but these seemingly imperfect beginnings actually hold the potential for future success. This is evident in various fields, such as Taobao, the 12,306 app, and the early military development of the Chinese Communist Party. Their success relied not only on having all production factors in place but also on leveraging core elements to address other deficiencies gradually (Fig. 13.2).

For example, Taobao initially had many low-quality products, but this did not prevent it from rapidly growing into a leading e-commerce platform in China and globally. This success stemmed from its mastery of key production elements in the internet era—platform development and rapid user accumulation. The strength of these core elements compensated for deficiencies in product quality and service experience, allowing Taobao to establish a foothold in a competitive market. Similarly, the 12,306 app initially did not support WeChat payments and had a poor user experience, but by monopolizing the crucial resource of ticket booking, it eventually became the main platform for railway tickets in China through continuous improvements.

While businesses do need multiple core elements for growth, not all elements need to be fully in place from the start. Companies at different stages should focus on priorities and strategies based on their specific situations. In the startup phase, emphasis should be on innovation and market development, with a strong leadership team, innovative capacity, and execution skills being particularly important. As the business grows, other factors like talent management, financial health, and corporate culture will become more prominent. Therefore, companies should focus on elements crucial for the current stage of development rather than striving for comprehensive perfection from the outset.

Different industries present varied challenges and opportunities. For example, tech companies may need to focus more on innovation and

Fig. 13.2 Rome wasn't built in a day. Many companies lack key elements in their early stages, but that doesn't prevent them from eventually achieving greatness

talent acquisition, while traditional manufacturing may prioritize cost control and operational efficiency. Companies should prioritize developing the most critical elements based on their industry and external environment, rather than aiming for perfection in all aspects from the beginning.

Business growth is a dynamic process, and the importance of different factors changes over time. For instance, early-stage companies may be more relaxed about financial management, focusing on market expansion and technological innovation. However, as the business grows, financial health and resource management become increasingly important. Therefore, businesses need to be adaptable in adjusting priorities to accommodate changes in internal and external environments.

Moreover, some elements have a complementary relationship. For example, an excellent leadership team and strong execution capabilities can compensate for initial financial resource shortages, while a robust corporate culture can help attract and retain top talent even with limited resources. Thus, companies do not need to excel in all areas; balancing development through core elements is more crucial.

Business growth is a process of continuous optimization and improvement. At different stages of development, certain elements may initially be incomplete, but through ongoing improvement and experience accumulation, companies can gradually enhance these elements. Startups might lack comprehensive policies for management and a strong culture, but these aspects can be strengthened through learning and adjustment over time.

In the process of business growth, encountering deficiencies or mistakes is inevitable. The key is whether a company can quickly adjust, learn from experiences, and continually improve. Adaptable and resilient companies, even with temporary shortcomings in certain elements, can gradually improve through practice, achieving long-term growth. Overall, business growth does not rely on having all core elements fully in place from the beginning. By prioritizing based on actual situations, focusing on breakthroughs, complementing each other, and continuously improving, companies can steadily achieve growth and expansion while gradually perfecting each element. Flexibility in responding to changes, continuous learning, and adjusting strategies are key to long-term success.

13.3 The Growth Story of Youth: The Dominant Role of Core Elements

Even though a child may initially have deficiencies in physical fitness, resistance, and intelligence, their greatest advantage lies in their capacity for learning and adaptation during the growth phase. These core elements play a dominant role in the growth process, helping to compensate for other shortcomings and allowing the child to become a future productive force.

A child's learning ability is their most significant strength. Research shows that a child's brain has high plasticity in the early stages, with the formation of neural connections occurring much faster than in adults. This neural plasticity enables children to rapidly absorb new knowledge, acquire skills, and adapt to changing environments. For example, infants can distinguish between different language sounds around six months of age, a feat challenging for adults. This learning ability allows children to quickly master basic skills like walking and talking, compensating for physical and intellectual shortcomings and gradually developing into well-rounded individuals.

Adaptability is another crucial advantage. Children can quickly adjust their behavior and thought processes when faced with new environments and challenges. Psychological research indicates that a child's brain can rapidly form new cognitive patterns in response to novel stimuli. For instance, children can flexibly adjust their social strategies in different social contexts, gradually mastering interpersonal skills. This adaptability not only helps them tackle challenges during growth but also fosters flexibility and creativity in the face of future uncertainties.

Another advantage bestowed by the growth phase is resilience and recovery. Studies have found that children have strong recovery abilities when facing difficulties, quickly bouncing back from failures and learning from experiences. For example, when learning to ride a bike, children may fall frequently in the beginning but continue to adjust and try again until they master the skill. This resilience and recovery ability allow children to overcome challenges during growth, turning adverse conditions into motivation for further development.

Through continuous learning and adaptation, children can improve physical fitness, enhance resistance, and boost intellectual levels. For instance, balanced nutrition and scientific exercise can gradually improve physical fitness, while education and cognitive development can enhance intellectual abilities.

The driving role of core elements allows children to compensate for their deficiencies during growth and ultimately become influential individuals in society. Learning and adaptability not only help them overcome growth challenges but also transform developmental potential into tangible outcomes, becoming carriers of new productivity. Many successful adults reflect on their growth process and acknowledge that it was through continuous learning and adaptation that they overcame early challenges and achieved personal success.

In summary, despite physical and intellectual shortcomings, a child's learning and adaptation abilities during growth enable them to gradually overcome these deficiencies and ultimately become significant new productive forces in society. These core elements not only stand strong on their own but also drive the improvement of other factors, ensuring notable success in future development.

13.4 Core Elements Driving Other Factors

The model of core elements driving development also applies in the high-tech field. For example, in 2024, China saw a surge in domestically produced humanoid robots, with several leading companies competing to release the latest products showcasing advanced flexibility and intelligence. However, compared to humanoid robots expected in the next 5 or 10 years, current products significantly lack stability and reliability. Although the demonstration videos highlight their impressive features, the actual reliability of these features still needs to be validated through long-term market testing and user feedback. It is inevitable that current humanoid robots do not possess final stability and reliability.

Nevertheless, these immature products are still favored by the market and investors. This is because they represent the future direction of technology and showcase significant potential. Market rewards often favor products with technological leadership, even if they are not yet mature, as this technological edge is a key factor in generating above-average profits in the current market. Other factors like management, sales channels, and supply chain efficiency, while important, often offer only average industry profits rather than excess profits in the early market phase.

In emerging markets, such as the nascent humanoid robot industry, technological leadership is crucial for success. Companies should focus resources on perfecting core technologies to gain a market-leading position. Although management and sales elements may still be developing in the early stages, profits from core technologies can gradually address these deficiencies. If companies prematurely focus on reducing costs and improving management efficiency during the technology dividend phase, they may miss the opportunity to secure excess profits from core technology, contradicting the strategies for early success (Fig. 13.3).

As time progresses, markets gradually mature, and supporting technologies continuously improve. In the future, humanoid robots might

Fig. 13.3 Dominant elements compensate for and supplement other deficiencies, allowing a seemingly makeshift troupe of a company to eventually overcome its shortcomings and become strong

become as easy to assemble as LEGO bricks, with corporate competition shifting more toward non-core technical aspects like management, sales channels, and user experience. However, in the early stages of the market, companies must seize the core element of technological leadership, maximizing the excess profits it brings to lay the foundation for future development. Just as a makeshift theater troupe attracts audiences with its brilliant performances, companies should focus on strengthening core technologies to stand out in a competitive market.

The development of any entity undergoes a transition from imperfection to maturity. In the initial stages, companies should concentrate resources on developing key production elements, using the excess profits they generate to gradually address other deficiencies. This approach allows companies to stand out in intense market competition and achieve long-term success. Thus, in the early stages of development, excessive pursuit of perfection across all aspects is counterproductive. Instead, accepting the reality of a "makeshift theater troupe" and focusing on core threshold elements, which in turn drive the development of other factors, is the key strategy for success in startups.

References

1. B. Singh, The Lean Startup: How Today's Entrepreneurs Use Continuous Innovation to Create Radically Successful Businesses, 2016.
2. P. Thiel and B. Masters, Zero to One: Notes on Startups, or How to Build the Future. Crown Currency, 2014.
3. C. M. Christensen, The Innovator's Dilemma: When New Technologies Cause Great Firms to Fail. Harvard Business Review Press, 2015.
4. J. Collins, Good to Great: Why Some Companies Make the Leap and Others Don't. Instaread, 2016.
5. S. Sinek, Start with Why: How Great Leaders Inspire Everyone to Take Action. Penguin, 2009.
6. M. Ganz, N. Nohria, and R. Khurana, "Leading Change," in Handbook of Leadership Theory and Practice: A Harvard Business School Centennial Colloquium. Harvard Business Review Press, 2010, pp. 527–568.
7. P. F. Drucker, "The Theory of the Business," Alfred P. Sloan: Critical Evaluations in Business and Management, vol. 2, no. 2, pp. 258–282, 1994.
8. M. E. Porter, Competitive Advantage: Creating and Sustaining Superior Performance. Simon and Schuster, 2008.
9. C. Christensen, M. E. Raynor, and R. McDonald, Disruptive Innovation. Harvard Business Review, 2013.

CHAPTER 14

Company Strategy Choices: Rapid Expansion vs. Quality Over Quantity

14.1 r/K Selection Theory in Ecology

The r/K selection theory is a key concept in ecology that explains differences in reproductive and survival strategies among species. In this theory, "r" represents the population growth rate, while "K" denotes the carrying capacity of the environment. It helps us understand why some species tend to reproduce rapidly, while others focus on the survival quality of each offspring. The core of the theory lies in environmental stability and resource availability.

The r-selection strategy, or "crazy breeding strategy," is suited for species living in unstable or unpredictable environments. These species increase their offspring's survival chances through rapid and prolific reproduction. For example, rodents, flies, and many fish are typical r-selected species. They produce a large number of offspring each time they reproduce, but the survival rate of each individual offspring is relatively low. The advantage of this strategy is its ability to quickly expand the population, especially during environmental upheavals, compensating for the high mortality rate of individual offspring through sheer numbers. This strategy is usually associated with shorter lifespans and smaller body sizes, with less parental care, relying on quantity to counter environmental challenges.

The K-selection strategy, or "quality over quantity strategy," applies to species living in resource-rich but competitive environments. Species like

X. Cao, *Modern Business Management*,
https://doi.org/10.1007/978-981-96-0594-1_14

elephants, whales, and humans represent this strategy. Their reproductive cycles are longer, producing fewer offspring at a time, but they invest significant care and attention in each offspring. The goal of this strategy is to ensure long-term population stability by increasing the survival rate of each offspring. K-selected species typically have longer lifespans and larger body sizes, focusing on the quality of individuals rather than quantity. Through meticulous parenting, these species gain survival advantages in environments with intense resource competition.

The r/K selection theory not only provides profound insights into species behavior in biology but can also be extended to fields such as economics and sociology, helping us understand how different individuals or organizations make survival and development decisions under limited resources. This theory illustrates the complexity and diversity of the biological world and reveals the broad scope of life's adaptability (Fig. 14.1).

14.2 r/K Selection Theory and Company Strategy Choices

In the business realm, the r/K selection theory provides a robust framework for companies to formulate their development strategies. According to this theory, companies can choose between r-selection strategies (rapid expansion) and K-selection strategies (refined development) based on market environment stability, resource availability, and competitive dynamics.

Unstable or Emerging Markets: For companies operating in rapidly changing or immature markets, such as new technology sectors or high-growth areas, the r-selection strategy is more suitable. In these environments, market conditions are not yet stable, and both opportunities and risks coexist. Companies need to quickly expand their business and increase market share to seize opportunities. For example, startups or growth-stage firms often adopt this strategy to establish a market presence and gain a competitive edge.

Stable or Mature Markets: If a company is in a mature market where competition is relatively stable and resources are limited, the K-selection strategy becomes more effective. In such environments, market growth is constrained, and companies should focus on enhancing product and service quality, strengthening brand value, and improving customer loyalty. This approach is suitable for mature companies or those in

Fig. 14.1 Mice and flies adopt the rapid expansion strategy, relying on "winning by numbers," they can quickly expand their populations in a short time, adapting to rapidly changing environments. In contrast, elephants, whales, and humans are typical quality over quantity strategists, meticulously nurturing and caring for each offspring to improve survival rates

high-end markets, emphasizing refined management and high-quality development to consolidate market position.

Resource-Rich: For companies with ample funding, technology, and human resources, the r-selection strategy might be more appropriate. These companies can quickly launch new products, enter new markets, or expand rapidly through mergers and acquisitions, aiming to capture market share. In this case, the focus is on quantity, aiming to expand influence rapidly in the short term.

Resource-Limited: When a company faces resource constraints or operates in a highly competitive industry with scarce resources, the K-selection strategy is more applicable. The company should concentrate resources on core business areas or high-potential markets, focusing on efficiency and quality to improve the success rate of each project or product. This strategy emphasizes optimizing internal processes and enhancing technological capabilities to gain a competitive advantage.

Intense Competition but Low Barriers to Entry: In highly competitive markets with low entry barriers, companies may need to adopt the r-selection strategy to fend off competitors. By engaging in extensive trial and error and rapid iteration, companies can find breakthroughs and seize market opportunities. For instance, internet startups often use this strategy to attract users through quick product iterations.

Limited Competition but High Barriers to Entry: For industries with limited competition but high entry barriers, companies can adopt the K-selection strategy. This involves focusing on innovation, technological advancement, and brand building, aiming to win the market with high-quality products and services. Such a strategy is suitable for industries requiring long-term investment and substantial accumulation, like high-tech, healthcare, or luxury markets.

Startup or Expansion Stage: During the startup or expansion phase, companies generally need to quickly capture market share to achieve economies of scale and brand recognition. In this stage, the r-selection strategy is more appropriate, focusing on rapidly expanding product lines and market coverage to gain a competitive advantage.

Mature Stage: As a company enters the mature stage, the marginal returns from market expansion decrease, and it should shift to the K-selection strategy. This involves optimizing internal management, maintaining customer relationships, and focusing on long-term brand development to ensure sustainable competitiveness.

In summary, when choosing between r-selection and K-selection strategies, companies should consider market environment stability, resource availability, competitive dynamics, and their own development stage. By accurately positioning themselves, companies can select the most suitable strategy to stand out in competitive markets.

14.3 Case Studies: Rapid Expansion vs. Quality and Sustainability

In the business world, companies often face the choice between two distinct development strategies: rapid expansion (r-selection strategy) and quality and sustainability (K-selection strategy). Each strategy offers unique advantages and challenges. Examining specific case studies can help illustrate how these strategies perform in various contexts.

The rapid expansion strategy emphasizes speed and market capture, aiming to establish market leadership through swift business growth. For instance, WeWork exemplifies this approach by rapidly expanding into numerous cities worldwide, striving to dominate the shared office space sector. Its success lies in quickly boosting brand recognition and market presence, attracting substantial investments and users. However, the high costs of expansion also brought significant financial strain, leading to management issues and cash flow problems that ultimately caused the company's difficulties.

Another example of the rapid expansion strategy is Uber. Since its inception, Uber has quickly expanded into major cities worldwide through massive subsidies and aggressive pricing strategies, achieving a leading position in the ride-hailing service sector. Uber later ventured into new areas such as food delivery and logistics. Although this strategy positioned Uber prominently in the global transportation market, it also led to ongoing financial strain and high cash burn. While effective in the early stages of market entry, this strategy can also present risks and challenges.

In contrast to the rapid expansion strategy, the quality and sustainability strategy focuses on long-term development and maintaining high standards. This approach requires companies to build market presence through steady growth and rigorous quality control. Apple Inc. is a prime example. Apple concentrates on innovating a limited range of core products, with each generation of iPhones and iPads meticulously designed and tested. This strategy has helped Apple build high brand loyalty and profitability, maintaining its leading position in the competitive tech market.

Another example of the quality and sustainability strategy is Patagonia, an outdoor clothing brand committed to environmental sustainability. Patagonia focuses on producing high-quality, eco-friendly products and selectively expanding its market. By emphasizing environmental and social responsibility, Patagonia has gained consumer trust and loyalty, achieving sustainable growth and maintaining long-term customer commitment in a competitive market.

In summary, the rapid expansion strategy is suited for situations where rapid market presence is crucial, especially in highly competitive early-stage industries. Conversely, the quality and sustainability strategy is more appropriate for companies focusing on long-term development and brand value. Companies should carefully consider their resources, market environment, and development goals when choosing a strategy to determine the most suitable path for growth.

14.4 Individual-Level Rapid Expansion vs. Quality and Sustainability Strategies

Choosing the right strategy is equally crucial for personal growth and career development. Individuals often face two distinct paths: rapid expansion and quality and sustainability strategies. These strategies represent different mindsets and approaches, each influencing personal success in various ways.

The rapid expansion strategy emphasizes broad experiences and quick actions. Those who adopt this strategy tend to seek diverse experiences and focus on breadth rather than depth. They believe that rapid action and varied attempts can lead to experience accumulation and opportunity discovery. For example, Elon Musk has ventured into various fields such as payments, space exploration, and energy. Despite the uncertainties in each area, his swift actions and flexible adjustments have led to significant success. Similarly, Richard Branson established a multinational business empire through adventurous ventures across multiple industries with the Virgin Group.

However, this strategy also carries risks. Rapid actions and widespread attempts can lead to scattered resources and burnout. Nonetheless, for those willing to take risks and explore, the rapid expansion strategy can provide rich experiences and unexpected opportunities (Fig. 14.2).

In contrast, the quality and sustainability strategy focuses on depth and preparation. This approach requires individuals to engage in thorough planning and reflection before taking action. Those who adopt this strategy emphasize quality over quantity, concentrating on a few areas and delving deeply into them. For example, Warren Buffett conducts extensive research before investing to ensure each investment is well-considered. His success stems from deep analysis and patiently waiting for the right

Fig. 14.2 The rapid expansion strategy solves problems through broad exploration and quick action, while the quality over quantity strategy addresses issues through careful nurturing and deep incubation

timing. Steve Jobs also exemplified the quality and sustainability strategy, refining product design to ensure each generation was flawless.

The advantage of the quality and sustainability strategy is its ability to provide steady success and reduce trial-and-error risks, though it requires more time and patience. Success often comes from deep expertise and meticulous preparation.

Whether in career development or personal growth, choosing the right strategy depends on individual personality traits and goals. For those who enjoy exploration, are action-oriented, and willing to take risks, the rapid expansion strategy may be more suitable. Conversely, for those who value stability, seek depth, and prefer thorough preparation before acting, the quality and sustainability strategy might be more appropriate. Understanding and choosing the strategy that fits one's own context is key to achieving goals and realizing dreams.

References

1. E. Ries, The Lean Startup: How Today's Entrepreneurs Use Continuous Innovation to Create Radically Successful Businesses. Crown Business, 2011.
2. P. Thiel, Zero to One: Notes on Startups, or How to Build the Future. Crown Business, 2014.
3. C. M. Christensen, The Innovator's Dilemma: When New Technologies Cause Great Firms to Fail. Harvard Business Review Press, 1997.
4. J. Collins, Good to Great: Why Some Companies Make the Leap… and Others Don't. HarperBusiness, 2001.
5. S. Sinek, Start with Why: How Great Leaders Inspire Everyone to Take Action. Penguin, 2009.
6. J. P. Kotter, Leading Change. Harvard Business Review Press, 1996.
7. P. F. Drucker, "The Theory of the Business," Harvard Business Review, vol. 72, no. 5, pp. 95–104, 1994.
8. M. E. Porter, Competitive Advantage: Creating and Sustaining Superior Performance. Free Press, 1985.
9. H. Chesbrough, Open Innovation: The New Imperative for Creating and Profiting from Technology. Harvard Business Review Press, 2003.
10. T. R. Eisenmann, Entrepreneurship: A Working Definition. Harvard Business School Working Paper, 2013.
11. C. M. Christensen, M. E. Raynor, and R. McDonald, "What Is Disruptive Innovation?" Harvard Business Review, vol. 93, no. 12, pp. 44–54, 2015.
12. A. S. Grove, Only the Paranoid Survive: How to Exploit the Crisis Points That Challenge Every Company and Career. Doubleday, 1996.

CHAPTER 15

Re-thinking the Theory of Evolution

15.1 Survival of the Fittest: The Fittest Are Not Necessarily the Strongest

Darwin's theory of evolution is centered on the principle of "natural selection" and "survival of the fittest," with the core idea being that it is not the strongest, smartest, or most excellent species that necessarily survive, but rather those that are best able to adapt to environmental changes. This same principle applies to the business world: some companies may not be the best in their industry, but they are able to adapt to changes in the environment, ultimately emerging as market leaders (Fig. 15.1).

Take Nokia and Apple as examples. The development histories of these two companies perfectly demonstrate the principle of "survival of the fittest." Nokia was once the undisputed leader in the global mobile phone market, with a market share that exceeded 40%. During the era of feature phones, Nokia won the favor of global users with its durable hardware, long battery life, and reliable quality. At that time, Nokia was undoubtedly a symbol of excellence. However, as the era of smartphones arrived, user needs changed significantly, and the market's expectations for mobile phones gradually shifted from durability to functionality, user experience, and the application ecosystem. In this new environment, Nokia failed to adjust its strategy in time, continuing to rely on its traditional strengths

X. Cao, *Modern Business Management*,
https://doi.org/10.1007/978-981-96-0594-1_15

Fig. 15.1 Darwin's theory of evolution illustrates the harsh survival competition in nature where natural selection determines survival

and ignoring the importance of smartphone operating systems and application ecosystems. On the other hand, Apple, with the launch of the iPhone, accurately grasped the new needs of smartphone users and introduced the iOS system with touchscreen operation, a powerful app store, and an excellent user experience. Although Apple has not always been at the forefront of hardware technology, its integration of software and hardware, along with its ecosystem construction, made its products more aligned with market demands, allowing it to quickly dominate the smartphone market. Ultimately, Nokia failed to adapt to the market upheaval and lost its leadership position, while Apple became the industry leader by adapting to market changes. This process perfectly exemplifies the concept that "survival of the fittest" does not necessarily mean "survival of the strongest."

Another classic example is the rise of Amazon. In the early days of the internet, companies like eBay and Yahoo performed exceptionally well in their respective fields—eBay almost monopolized the online auction space, while Yahoo was one of the most popular portals. However, these companies failed to adapt well to the rapid changes in the internet industry. eBay was overly reliant on its auction model and did not transition quickly enough to fixed-price retail. Yahoo failed to continue innovating in the search engine field and was eventually overtaken by Google. In contrast, Amazon, which started as an online bookstore, gradually expanded into almost every retail sector. Through its excellent supply chain management, innovative logistics systems, and extreme focus on user experience, Amazon gradually adapted to the various changes and challenges of e-commerce. Today, Amazon is not only the world's largest e-commerce platform but also a giant in cloud computing, artificial intelligence, and other fields. This success is rooted in Amazon's high adaptability to environmental changes rather than its absolute dominance in any single area.

Darwin's theory of evolution—"natural selection, survival of the fittest"—applies equally well to the business world. A company's success does not necessarily depend on its absolute advantage at any given moment but rather on its ability to adjust its strategy in response to market and environmental changes, maintaining high adaptability. The examples of Nokia and Apple, eBay and Amazon, clearly demonstrate that those companies that can quickly adapt to changes and meet market demands are the true survivors and winners.

15.2 The 35-Year-Old Crisis for Technologists

In career development, we often hear about the "35-year-old crisis," especially in the technology sector. Many students who performed well in university and chose technical positions after graduation face the risk of being phased out by the time they reach 35. Meanwhile, those who were average students in university and reluctantly chose after-sales or sales positions upon graduation may find themselves reaching the peak of their careers in middle age due to early transitions into management roles. This phenomenon is rooted in profound career logic, echoing Darwin's theory of "survival of the fittest."

The core of technical positions lies in technology itself. The rapid pace of technological innovation requires practitioners to constantly learn and master the latest skills. However, as individuals age, their ability and energy to learn new technologies inevitably decline. This means that even highly skilled technologists in their youth may face severe challenges around the age of 35: new technologies quickly replace old ones, and if technologists cannot keep up with these changes, they risk losing their competitiveness (Fig. 15.2).

In contrast, the core of management positions is the management of people and resources, involving complex factors such as human nature, teamwork, and organizational culture. While management skills and methods also need updating, the rate of change is much slower than in the technology field. More importantly, management experience and understanding of human nature become increasingly valuable over time. Therefore, those who transition from technical roles to management early on, although they may not appear "excellent" at the start, tend to become more competitive in management positions as time passes.

We can better understand this by looking at the career trajectories of university classmates. In computer science or information technology majors, the students who perform best often choose technical roles after graduation, thriving in the technical field due to their solid technical foundations. However, classmates who were average in school and less proficient in technology often choose after-sales, sales, or other positions less closely related to technology upon graduation. Over time, these average students gradually transition into management roles, accumulating management experience. Ten or fifteen years later, the once

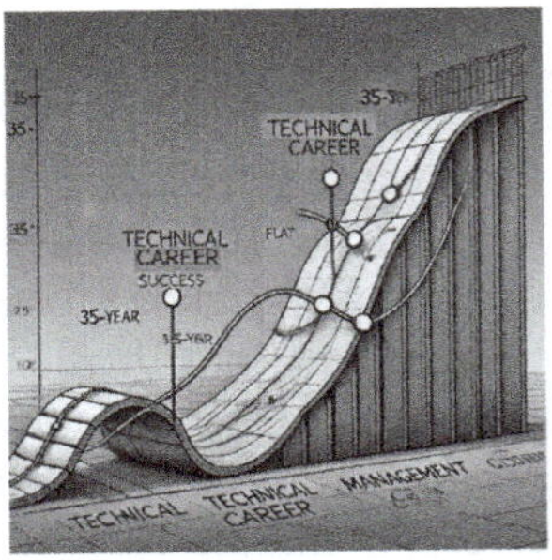

Fig. 15.2 The 35-year-old crisis

top-performing students who remained in technical roles may face challenges such as outdated technical knowledge and difficulty learning new technologies, feeling career bottlenecks, or even the threat of layoffs at 35. On the other hand, those who transitioned into management early, having accumulated rich experience, gradually mastered the ability to manage teams and resources, and now have become the backbone of the enterprise, with their careers flourishing.

This phenomenon can be likened to sickle cell anemia in biology. Under normal circumstances, sickle cell anemia is a genetic mutation that leads to abnormally shaped red blood cells with reduced oxygen-carrying capacity, considered a disadvantage. However, in malaria-endemic regions, this mutation becomes an advantage because these abnormal red blood cells make it difficult for the malaria parasite to survive in the body, giving individuals with this genetic mutation greater survival ability in a malarial environment. This "inherent defect" turning into an advantage in specific environments is strikingly similar to the career trajectory of "average" students who transitioned early into management roles.

These examples demonstrate that career success is not always determined by being "excellent" at the starting point but by the ability to adapt to environmental changes over time. Technologists, if they can transition to management roles at the right time in their careers, can accumulate experience and gain an advantage in middle age. Conversely, those who remain on a purely technical path, despite starting from a high point, may face increasing challenges as technology evolves rapidly, even risking obsolescence.

This again verifies Darwin's theory of "survival of the fittest"—in career development, the ability to adapt to environmental changes is more important than initial excellence. Those who can flexibly adjust their career paths according to the environment and personal circumstances often emerge as the winners in a competitive job market.

15.3 Artificial Evolution and Franchising

In the theory of evolution, there is a concept called "artificial selection," which refers to the process by which humans, through intervention, selectively breed certain biological traits, thereby guiding the development of certain species. This artificial evolution differs from natural selection, which eliminates individuals that cannot adapt to their environment, while artificial selection is human-driven, protecting and breeding species with specific values, even if those species lack competitive advantages in the natural environment. This phenomenon exists not only in biological evolution but can also be likened to certain enterprises in the business world.

Take the fainting goat as an example. Due to a genetic mutation, this type of goat faints from muscle spasms when startled, making them easy prey for predators. From the perspective of natural selection, these goats have no survival advantage and should be naturally eliminated over time. However, humans discovered that fainting goat meat is exceptionally tender, so they provided these goats with a safe and comfortable living environment, protecting them from predators. Through human care, these goats, which might have disappeared in the wild, not only avoided extinction but also thrived worldwide due to the deliciousness of their meat, becoming a popular species.

Another example is the goldfish. Goldfish originated from common carp, but through long-term artificial selection and breeding, they became the species we know today. Goldfish are slow-moving and have a hard time evading predators in the wild, meaning they would have little survival advantage. However, because goldfish have high ornamental value, humans have continuously selectively bred them and provided them with artificial breeding environments, making them a prosperous species (Fig. 15.3).

In the business world, some companies, while lacking significant competitiveness in the free market, have unique resources or franchise rights in certain industries, allowing them to dominate the competition. This situation is similar to the way fainting goats and goldfish thrive in specific artificial environments.

The tobacco industry is a good example. In many countries, tobacco production and sales are strictly regulated, usually granted as a franchise by the government. Companies involved in these industries might not be able to compete with more innovative or efficient companies in a free market. However, due to government protection and franchise rights, these companies can operate monopolistically in specific markets, continuing to generate profits. It is this "artificial selection" market environment that gives these companies a "survival advantage" akin to that of fainting goats and goldfish in biological terms.

Another example is the high entry barriers in certain high-tech industries. Some industries require substantial technical expertise, capital, and

Fig. 15.3 The unusual evolution of fainting goats and goldfish is the result of artificial selection

intellectual property, limiting the number of companies that can enter and compete. For instance, industries like aerospace and nuclear energy have high technical barriers and strict market entry regulations, meaning only companies with special resources and technical capabilities can participate. This unique market environment allows these companies, even if less competitive in other markets, to attain a high market position and profit in specific industries.

In both biological evolution and business competition, the ability to adapt to specific environments often outweighs general competitive ability. In nature, species that might lack a survival advantage can thrive if they possess certain valuable traits that humans protect and breed. Similarly, in the business world, companies that may not have outstanding competitiveness in a free market can find unique opportunities for development due to special resources, franchise rights, or strict market entry barriers. Just as species thrive in artificially created environments, these companies prosper due to specific market conditions, becoming giants in their industries.

15.4 The Driving Force of Evolution

Darwin's theory of evolution is centered on "survival competition," proposing a mechanism for biological evolution driven by competition. He pointed out that competition among living organisms drives species evolution, but he initially could not explain why this competition occurs or what its objective basis is. It was not until he read Malthus's Essay on the Principle of Population that he found the answer. Malthus pointed out that population growth is exponential, while the resources supporting population survival can only grow at a linear rate. This mismatch leads to resource scarcity, triggering survival competition.

In nature, resources are limited. Whether it is food, water, or habitat, all species rely on these limited resources to survive. Due to the strong reproductive ability of organisms, population numbers would grow exponentially if not externally restricted. However, the resources needed to sustain these organisms grow at a linear rate, inevitably leading to resource shortages. When resources cannot meet the needs of all organisms, competition becomes inevitable. In this competition, not all individuals survive. Those better able to adapt to environmental changes and utilize resources more effectively have a greater chance of survival and reproduction. Those who cannot adapt to the environment fail in the competition and may even be eliminated. Darwin's "survival of the fittest" theory is based on this logic, explaining why there is such fierce survival competition in the biological world (Fig. 15.4).

This mechanism of survival competition applies not only to the natural world but can also be likened to the business world. In the business world, many entrepreneurs emerge from existing companies. Suppose each year, 1% of company employees choose to start their own businesses; this 1% can be seen as the "birth rate" of the business world. When the economy is active, entrepreneurial enthusiasm is high, and new companies spring up

Fig. 15.4 Darwin's theory of survival of the fittest and Malthus's population theory are equally applicable in the business world. The conflict between limited resources and unlimited demand, market competition among enterprises, and the concept of "survival of the fittest" together create the conditions for successful companies to stand out in competition

like mushrooms after rain—this increase in the number of companies is similar to the exponential growth of populations in the biological world.

However, the resources and opportunities driving economic growth are not infinite. While productivity and technological advances can lead to growth, this growth is usually linear. Compared to the rapidly increasing number of companies, market demand, customer resources, and technological dividends grow at a relatively slower pace. This imbalance leads to fierce competition in the business world. When the economy enters a recession, this competition becomes even more brutal. Just as organisms face survival challenges when resources are scarce in nature, during economic downturns, market demand decreases, funding tightens, customers are lost, and competition among companies intensifies, ultimately leading to many companies going out of business. Only those companies most capable of adapting to environmental changes and flexibly responding to market challenges can survive.

The companies that survive this competition are not necessarily the most ethical or the most technologically advanced. They may compromise on business ethics, be less than exemplary in paying taxes, or not be leaders in cutting-edge technology. But they stand out in the competition because they possess the adaptability required by the environment at the time. Whether through flexible business strategies, sharp market instincts, or effective cost control, these companies demonstrate strong adaptability in fierce competition. After achieving success, these companies often rebrand themselves to align with public moral standards and aesthetic expectations, striving to present the image of a "successful enterprise." However, the core truth remains that these companies survive and grow primarily because they exhibit outstanding adaptability in specific business environments.

Darwin's theory of survival competition, grounded in Malthus's population theory, finds its objective basis in the contradiction between the limited availability of resources and the infinite demand for them. The same logic applies to the business world—linear economic and resource growth cannot keep pace with the exponential growth in the number of companies, leading to intense market competition. In this competition, only those companies most capable of adapting to environmental changes survive. These companies are not necessarily the most ethical or technologically advanced, but they stand out as examples of "survival of the fittest" in the fierce competition. Just as species adapt to their environment through evolution, successful companies in the business world evolve as winners in the market competition.

References

1. C. Darwin, On the Origin of Species by Means of Natural Selection. Good Press, 2023.
2. J. M. Smith and E. Szathmáry, The Major Transitions in Evolution. Oxford University Press, 1997.
3. A. Gardner and J. J. Welch, "A Formal Theory of the Selfish Gene," Journal of Evolutionary Biology, vol. 24, no. 8, pp. 1801–1813, 2011.
4. S. Pinker, The Better Angels of Our Nature: The Decline of Violence in

History and Its Causes. Penguin UK, 2011.
5. G. C. Williams, Adaptation and Natural Selection: A Critique of Some Current Evolutionary Thought. Princeton University Press, 2018.
6. E. O. Wilson, Sociobiology: The New Synthesis. Harvard University Press, 2000.
7. G. Abatecola, F. Belussi, D. Breslin, et al., "Darwinism, Organizational Evolution and Survival: Key Challenges for Future Research," Journal of Management & Governance, vol. 20, pp. 1–17, 2016.
8. S. Jofre, Exploring the Role of Knowledge and Technology Transfer in Innovation Systems, in Triple Helix IX International Conference: "Silicon Valley: Global Model or Unique Anomaly?" Stanford University Press, 2011.
9. R. A. Burgelman, M. A. Maidique, and S. C. Wheelwright, Strategic Management of Technology and Innovation. Irwin, 1996.
10. A. D. Chandler and T. Hikino, Scale and Scope: The Dynamics of Industrial Capitalism. Harvard University Press, 2009.
11. A. M. Hjalager, "A Review of Innovation Research in Tourism," Tourism Management, vol. 31, no. 1, pp. 1–12, 2010.
12. M. A. Schilling, Strategic Management of Technological Innovation. McGraw-Hill, 2017.

Epilogue

A poem to express the sentiment after completing this book manuscript:

The Tide of Involution, The Way to Break Through
In the surging tides of the times,
The market is like a torrent, surging endlessly.
Monopolies stand like towering mountains,
Emerging companies seek survival in the gaps.
Capital flows like the sea, supply chains are like webs,
Traditional giants control the pulse of the times.
Small advantages magnify over time,
The power of compounding widens the gap infinitely.
But the dark horses do not stop at obstacles,
Galloping through segmented tracks.
Like species in evolution,
They break old chains with innovation.
The heartbeat of life beats rapidly,
A brief prosperity flashes like lightning.
The rhythm of birth and death,
Is written in the fast-changing market.
With slow overcoming the fast, deep cultivation,
In seemingly lonely niches, they move stealthily.
One day, gold will shine,
Standing out in the market competition.
Deep accumulation, persistence,
Seeking answers in long-termism.

X. Cao, *Modern Business Management*,
https://doi.org/10.1007/978-981-96-0594-1

No matter how fierce the storm, how perilous the market,
Only those who persevere can ultimately triumph.
This is the revelation of the era of involution,
Finding a way to break through in fierce competition.
May this book guide you,
Finding light in moments of confusion.

The writing and completion of this book could not have been possible without the support of advanced technology. Notably, the images used in this book were all generated through ChatGPT. This process utilized the latest artificial intelligence technology, ensuring that the images accurately convey the core ideas and concepts of the content. This not only demonstrates the powerful capabilities of AI in image generation but also allows this book to be presented to readers in a more intuitive and rich manner.

I sincerely hope that these innovative technologies will enhance your reading experience and look forward to continuing to explore and apply more technological means to present even more exciting content to you in the future. Thank you to every reader for your support and attention, and may we together navigate the ocean of knowledge, welcoming more challenges and opportunities.

Index

A
Adaptation, vi, 16, 121–123
Artificial intelligence (AI), 19, 43, 47, 48, 51, 63, 67, 75, 83, 89, 101, 105, 106, 109, 137, 148

B
Business ecosystems, 114
Business strategy, 93, 144

C
Capital accumulation, 2, 3, 80
Compounding effect, 3, 5–8
Concentration, 5, 8, 10, 23–25, 27, 98, 100
Corporate strategy, 48

D
Deep cultivation, 17–21
Dinosaur extinction, 79, 80, 85
Diversification, 23–31

E
Economies of scale, 3, 130
Environmental change, v, 82, 85, 86, 135, 137, 139, 142, 144
Evolution theory, v

H
Human desires, 61–64

I
Incremental growth, 79, 80, 82

K
Key Performance Indicators (KPIs), vi, 33–41

L
Lifespan-Heartbeat Hypothesis, 13–16
Long-termism, vi, 20, 21

X. Cao, *Modern Business Management*,
https://doi.org/10.1007/978-981-96-0594-1

M

Market competition, v, vi, 16, 19, 43, 44, 46–48, 93, 106, 125, 143, 144
Metabolic rate, 13
Moore's Law, 59–64, 67

N

Natural selection, 74, 135–137, 139, 140
Niche markets, vi, 7–10

O

Objectives and Key Results (OKRs), vi, 33–41
Overstaffing, 45, 46

P

Price wars, 3, 6, 47, 48
Profit margins, 3–5, 7, 9, 10, 33, 39, 44–49, 83

R

r/K selection theory, 127, 128
Rapid Expansion vs. Quality and Sustainability, 131, 132
Research and development (R&D), 5, 35, 38, 39, 41, 46–49
Risk management, 25

S

Shrinking resources, 81, 82
Strategic adjustments, 37
Supply chain management, 36, 44, 47, 48, 137
Survival of the fittest, v, 135, 137–139, 142–144

T

Technological barriers, vi, 5
Technological innovation, v, 44–48, 112, 121, 138
Tertiary industry, 51, 53

W

Winner-takes-all, v, 1, 3, 5–8